"A GREAT DEAL OF GENTLE WISDOM AND HUMOR . . .

MAYBE (MAYBE NOT) deserves a place on your bedside table."

—*Nashville Banner*

"What Fulghum does, with amusing and heart-warming anecdotes from his own life, is remind us of everyday truths. It's commonsense stuff, and there's certainly nothing wrong with that."

—*The Indianapolis Star*

"The revelations of learning to iron a shirt, listening to his elders swap tales at the barbershop, contemplating the circumstances of one's own conception and other musings reveal a glimpse of a simpler life where, maybe, we can slow down and enjoy the fullness of life as it's meant to be."

—*The Charleston Post & Courier*

"Light, charming, page-turning fare, with plenty to be read aloud and recalled with pleasure."

—*The Anniston Star*

"Fulghum writes about what goes on behind the closed door of the secret side of our minds. . . . [He] is always a pleasure to read. . . . Some readers may want to use lightly penciled marginal notes to help them return quickly to particular favorites."

—*Austin American-Statesman*

Also by Robert Fulghum
Published by Ballantine Books:

UH-OH
IT WAS ON FIRE WHEN I LAY DOWN ON IT
ALL I REALLY NEED TO KNOW I LEARNED IN
   KINDERGARTEN

Maybe
(Maybe Not)

Second Thoughts from a Secret Life

Robert Fulghum

IVY BOOKS • NEW YORK

An Ivy Book
Published by The Random House Publishing Group
Copyright © 1993 by Robert Fulghum

Published in the United States by Ivy Books, an imprint of The Random House Publishing Group, a division of Random House, Inc., New York, and simultaneously in Canada by Random House of Canada Limited, Toronto.

Library of Congress Catalog Card Number: 92-56811

ISBN 0-8041-1115-4

This edition published by arrangement with Villard Books, a division of Random House, Inc., New York. Villard Books is a registered trademark of Random House, Inc.

Manufactured in the United States of America

www.ballantinebooks.com

First Ballantine Books Edition: May 1995

OPM   19   18   17   16   15   14   13   12   11

A RABBI AND I ONCE ENGAGED IN A FRIENDLY INtellectual hockey match trying to choose a single word to summarize human wisdom. He submitted a Hebrew term—*timshel*. It's found in the oldest story in our common literature—in Genesis—the book of beginnings.

After being expelled from the Garden of Eden, Adam and Eve had two sons. The elder was called Cain. He was the first man born outside of paradise.

In time Cain grew up and cultivated his land and brought the first fruits as an offering to God. The offering was rejected. Jehovah explained to Cain that he was tangled up with evil—it lurked around his door. "But," Jehovah said, "you may triumph over evil and have abundant life."

That's a crucial sentence—the last thing Jehovah says to Cain.

"You *may* triumph over evil and have abundant life."

The critical word is the second one, the verb— *may*.

Timshel in Hebrew.

This term has vexed scholars and theologians for a long time. It sits in the middle of a passage considered one of the five most difficult in the Scriptures to translate and understand. In context it has varied meanings, especially in this interchange between Jehovah and Cain.

Timshel has been interpreted to mean "you shall"—that's an order, a command. *Timshel* has been interpreted to mean "you will"—which implies predestination. *Timshel* has even been interpreted to mean "you cannot," which suggests hopeless dependence. All these interpretations define a relationship with God that leaves little freedom.

My friend the rabbi feels that the practical meaning of that passage of Scripture concerns vitality—meaning "Don't be dead," or "Don't be a passive victim—be active—be alive." He reads it as good advice: There is this problem with evil— you really *should* deal with it.

Carry that one step further—if you *should*, then you *may*.

To interpret *timshel* to mean "you may" is to use

a word that implies the possibility of choice. This is not a matter of theological hairsplitting. I think a strong case can be made that human beings have at least acted *as if* "you may" was the correct interpretation—acting *as if* our destiny is in our hands.

Whatever we may think or believe, what we have *done* is our story.

You don't need to be a theologian or belong to any particular religious group to enter this discussion, but you do come down somewhere on this issue of what's possible in your life by how you in fact go about your life. You live this truth, one way or another.

In modern English, *timshel* means "it may be," or, simply, "maybe."

Maybe. There's our word.

The wisest answer to ultimate questions.

A word pointing at open doors and wide horizons.

I do not believe that the meaning of life is a puzzle to be solved.

Life is. I am. Anything might happen.

And I believe I *may* invest my life with meaning.

The uncertainty is a blessing in disguise.

If I were absolutely certain about all things, I would spend my life in anxious misery, fearful of losing my way. But since everything and anything are always possible, the miraculous is always nearby and wonders shall never, ever cease.

I believe that human freedom may be stated in one term, which serves as a little brick propping open the door of existence: Maybe.

*S*UPPOSE THAT EVERYTHING GOING ON IN YOUR HEAD in twenty-four hours could be accurately recorded on videotape. Your night dreams and daytime fantasies, conversations with yourself and appeals to the gods, the music and memories that float about, and all the loony trivia that ricochets around in your mind.

Suppose all this material could be played in a theater—with multiple screens and a multitrack sound system. A pretty sensational show, I'd guess. MTV, X-rated video, Science Fiction Theater, Harlequin Romances, CD-ROM, and the *National Enquirer* combined couldn't compete with what goes on behind the closed door of the secret side of our minds.

The operative word here is *"secret."*

Public lives are lived out on the job and in the marketplace, where certain rules, conventions, laws, and social customs keep most of us in line.

Private lives are lived out in the presence of family, friends, and neighbors who must be considered and respected, even though the rules and proscriptions are looser than what's allowed in public.

But in our *secret* lives, inside our own heads, almost anything goes.

We alone are answerable for what we think and do when nobody else is around or involved. Categories of "fact" and "fiction" are irrelevant in here. Are dreams true? Is what you imagine accurate?

Inside these tight boundaries of flesh and bone is a borderless jungle in which clearings exist. In these open spaces, there may be an amusement park, a zoo, a circus, a library, a museum, a theater, or a landscape stranger than Mars.

We refer to ourselves in first person singular— "I"—but inside, it's more like first person plural. Most of the time, my inner life seems like a ventriloquist act. A ceaseless dialogue between Me and my dummy. Oddly enough, the dummy is smarter than I am.

It seems as if my dummy and I have lots of company. There's quite a crowd in here with us. A child and its parents. A wise old person. A mechanic, demons, a fool, a scientist, comedian, musician, dancer, athlete, magician, professor; a Romeo, censor, police officer, fire fighter, and multitudes more. The population of a small town inhabits the landscape of these disunited states of myself. And the town meeting is always in session.

I can fully relate to the occasional stories in the tabloids about multiple personalities. This is not news to me. In the best sense of the word, I run an asylum—a safe refuge—in my mind. And it's not a problem. As long as I keep the shades drawn and the doors closed, and don't let anybody loose, all is well. As long as I'm firmly in charge of my secret life, the world sees me as sane and functional. Am I? Sometimes it's hard to tell.

Those who have closely considered the secret life—people like Freud and Jung—use metaphors to speak about the way we keep the secret life from causing chaos in personal and public life. They speak of "the gatekeeper," "superego," "monitor," and "inner parent."

My own metaphor is *the Committee.*

And my ventriloquist's dummy seems to be the chairman.

I think of my committee as odds makers who say things like, "If you rob a bank, it's ten to one that the FBI will get you, and you will end up in jail for a long time." Or, "If you tell people you talk to God, they'll think you're religious, but if you say God talks to you, it's ten to one they'll think you're crazy."

* * *

Most of the time, most of us go around with our heads running full tilt doing the most amazing things, while we safely negotiate the obligations of public and private life. Much of what goes on in the secret life is not aberrational. Sometimes entertaining, it is often mundane and unexceptional—neither dramatic nor demonic. Just the necessary backstage maintenance operation of life where we sort out the contradictory material into piles of what works and what doesn't, what's useful and what's not.

The French have a charming term for one aspect of the secret life.

La perruque. It means "the wig," and is slang for a particular kind of disguise. It refers to what you do for yourself while apparently going about the job you are paid to do. If you are a typist working at your desk and you are in fact writing a letter to your lover on company time, this is *la perruque.* When you make personal calls from your office phone, do a little grocery shopping while out on company business, daydream, or even use your employer's time to make a list of things to do over the weekend, it's all *la perruque*—conducting your personal life under the guise of working at your job. It's not stealing. It's an acknowledgment that your *public* life, *personal* life, and *secret* life run concurrently and parallel. *La perruque* on the job is balanced by the time you think about work while you are on vacation.

* * *

The workings of a family include the secret life.

My oldest son is a man now. Thirty-two, grown-up. He knows about money, sex, love, work—success and failure. We have become peers in many ways.

We went out for a beer together recently, and he confessed to me things he thought and did behind my back when he was a kid. Then I confessed to him things I knew he was thinking and doing but didn't do anything about because I couldn't deal with them, having done the same or worse when I was his age. While playing the public role of parent, I was still secretly both a rebellious adolescent and a fearful child. *La perruque*—always the disguises.

Or consider this family secret.

The father of a friend died suddenly at eighty-two. My friend was an only child, himself divorced, and his own children lived too far away to come to the funeral. A lonely time.

The father was a solemn, humorless, literal-minded man who had been a mechanical engineer all his life. Not much imagination or affection. My friend respected his father, but the relationship was a formal and somewhat distant one. But now his father was dead, and the son was the sole heir to the estate.

The government thinks of an estate as money, stocks, bonds, life insurance, jewelry, and any other tangible item of value that can be assessed and taxed. But there is always all the other stuff—all the small things—the knickknacks—the odds and ends of a life. These are kept, sometimes hidden, in places where you would not ever trespass when your parents were alive. But now you must look. And make decisions about what to keep and what to dispose of. You are licensed by death to enter the antechamber of your parents' secret life.

There is usually a drawer. Top drawer. In a bureau in the bedroom.

In this case, the father was an orderly man. At one end of his top drawer were all his socks, folded and sorted by color—black and brown. In the other end, several small boxes and a tobacco tin.

In one little box, his U.S. Air Force insignia pins from his uniform and cap. In another, miscellaneous jewelry—tie tacks, collar stays, studs, some foreign coins, and three keys. The old man kept his deceased wife's wedding ring in the original box from the jewelers, along with a lock of her red hair.

And in a flat cigar tin, wrapped in tissue paper, there were tiny teeth neatly glued to a card, with a date under each one in the father's handwriting. Human teeth.

This find was a bit of a shock.

His *father* was the *tooth fairy*.

All these years he'd thought it was his mom.

Not all the family secrets are bad news.

WHEN MY GROWN CHILDREN CONFESS WHAT THEY did behind my back when they were kids, it doesn't occur to them that I was also doing a few things behind their backs. In the spirit of fairness to my wife and children, I confess:

I used the wok once to change the oil in the car.
And I used the sewing scissors to cut canvas.
I used the kitchen-sink sponge to clean my shoes.
Sometimes I said the coffee I made was decaf when it wasn't.
Yes, it was me who ate the baking chocolate.
The hamsters didn't die from old age.
I deliberately left price tags on presents sometimes. Even raised them.

11

I always took a private cut of the money Grandmother sent for Christmas.

I lied when I said you looked beautiful when you were a teenager.

When I did the cooking, what I said wasn't leftovers often was.

The *Playboy* subscription that came for years was not a gift from a friend.

Remember when all the old white underwear got stained pink in the wash? It wasn't an accident.

I know who sent you anonymous cards for Valentine's Day.

I know who took money out of my wallet.

But I know you know who took money out of the piggy banks.

At times I said I missed you when, in fact, I was glad to be alone for a while.

I always said I was proud of you—even when I knew you could do better.

I let you lie to me sometimes because the truth was too hard for all of us.

Sometimes I said "I love you" when I didn't love anyone, not even me.

Your mother and I both played Santa Claus on Christmas Eve.

But I was always the Easter Bunny.

*A*T THE END OF JANUARY, AT THE END OF MY DESK, sits a potted poinsetta.

Yes, I know that the correct spelling and pronunciation are "poinsettia."

I don't care.

And I am trying hard not to care about this particular plant.

For my role in its life is that of executioner.

Every year in December for as long as I can remember, at least one potted poinsetta has appeared in my life. I never buy one. Someone always gives me one. Unlike other seasonal gift flowers—lilies, daffodils, carnations, and such—poinsettas do not just bring their message and then die and leave your life in a graceful way. They have a life span comparable to a sea turtle, and are as tenacious as cacti. Even if neglected, they will hang on and on and on. Encouraged, they can become bushes sixteen feet high.

Do you know how these things got into the holiday package in the first place? Joel Roberts Poinsett is to blame. He lived from 1779 to 1851 and spent his life as a South Carolina politician—elected first to the U.S. Congress and serving most of the rest of his life as a diplomatic envoy to various countries south of the border, most notably Mexico. Poinsett was a manipulative sort, and he managed to meddle in Mexican politics so often that he was officially declared persona non grata. The Mexicans coined the word *poinsettismo* to characterize his kind of intrusive behavior.

When Poinsett returned to the United States, he brought a flowering plant with him, formally labeled *Euphorbia pulcherrima*, but popularly called "poinsettia" in his honor. Its winter foliage of red and green leaves quickly gave it a place of honor in our Christmas traditions. And a place of nuisance in January. As I contemplate the potted plant on my desk, I comprehend the personal meaning of *poinsettismo*—this problematic plant intrudes upon my life.

If my wife had her way, we would have kept every poinsetta that ever entered our domicile. Our house would become a poinsetta refuge. Lynn the Good

14

would not knowingly end the life of any living thing. It does no good to explain to her that poinsettas are not puppies. And she can't stand leaving them neglected around the house while they slowly wither and expire. She covertly waters them when I am out of the house. In times past, we had poinsettas struggling on into July. We have finally agreed that "something" had to happen to poinsettas, but she doesn't want to know exactly what.

As usual, my lot is being the family criminal. I do the dirty deeds. Exterminate bugs and mice, throw out wilting flowers, and empty the refrigerator of mummified leftovers. And make the poinsettas disappear.

At her insistence, I did try a few humane tactics. But I learned that giving away a poinsetta in January is like trying to unload zucchini in August. Neither the neighbors nor the Salvation Army had any interest. Leaving one on a bench at a bus stop in hopes it would be adopted didn't work. The poinsetta was still there three days later. My wife rescued it and brought it home again. Tossing it in a nearby Dumpster brought the same result.

I tried to interest her in a ceremony called "the Setting Free of the Poinsetta." This involved taking the plant out of the pot, lowering it reverently off our dock into the water, and letting it float away on the lake. Maybe the wildlife would eat some of it, and the rest would blend into the great cycle of decay and return of which all living things are part. An organic solution with cosmic overtones. But a bird-watching friend told us the plant was toxic to waterfowl. Those pretty red leaves are poisonous.

One year I left a poinsetta outside in the falling snow. It looked so nice out there—and an easy way to go. If it couldn't handle the cold, so be it. We still had it in March.

We've finally settled on an unspoken plan where one unannounced day in January I will surreptitiously pick up the poinsetta as I'm going out the door. I carry the poinsetta off to my office, where it will live for a while until it dies. The janitor tosses it out. And that's that. Easy.

Well, not quite.

In truth, in my secret life, I am of two minds on this subject.

As in many cases, something that may be trivial may also be important.

Part of me thinks I should be on the side of anything so beautiful that hangs on to life without much help from me. It brings vibrancy to winter's gloom. And will outlive me with only an occasional watering. I should hold poinsettas in esteem and have them planted on my grave.

And another side of me says to hold back on the heavy thinking. These things are dispensable holiday decorations. No metaphorical anthropomorphic thinking need apply. A poinsetta is a potted plant, not a paradigm of existence. When its usefulness is served, it goes to the dump. Come on.

It was looking droopy when I came in this morning.

So. I watered it.

Not a lot. I don't want to encourage the thing too much.

Maybe it will expire over the weekend. Maybe not.

*T*HAT AMBIVALENCE OVER THE FATE OF A POINSETTA is typical of the way I often think. Despite the apparent ability to make decisions and get on with my business, the inside of my head is kaleidoscopic every time I shake it, there seems to be a new picture. A distant relative reports that the motto written on our family crest is *"Soyez ferme"*—"be firm." That's a laugh. For me, in my secret life, the real motto is *"Forsan, non forsan."* Maybe, maybe not.

I once began a list of the contradictory notions I hold:

Look before you leap.
He who hesitates is lost.

19

Two heads are better than one.
If you want something done right, do it yourself.

Nothing ventured, nothing gained.
Better safe than sorry.

Out of sight, out of mind.
Absence makes the heart grow fonder.

You can't tell a book by its cover.
Clothes make the man.

Many hands make light work.
Too many cooks spoil the broth.

You can't teach an old dog new tricks.
It's never too late to learn.

Never sweat the small stuff.
God is in the details.

And so on. The list goes on forever. Once I got so caught up in this kind of thinking that I wore two buttons on my smock when I was teaching art. One said, "Trust me, I'm a teacher." The other replied, "Question Authority."

The Viennese have a word for the ability to carry on the business of daily life despite the bipolarities. *Fortwursteln*—a term that means getting by for long periods on little sausages and small potatoes. The word is also a reference to Hans Wurst, the male clown of Punch-and-Judy shows, whose specialty is confusion and the avoidance of big decisions. *Fortwursteln* refers to the ability to cope and muddle on—to function between maybe and maybe not.

I think about this dichotomy when I visit a special place in our nation's capital. At the west end of Constitution Avenue in Washington, D.C., screened from the street by a grove of elm and holly trees, there sits a memorial statue. A portrayal in bronze of Albert Einstein.

Twenty-one feet tall, seated on a three-step bench of white granite, Einstein is depicted here in comfort—dressed in a baggy sweater, wrinkled corduroy trousers, and sandals, his hair in its familiar disarray. His face reflects a combination of wisdom, tranquillity, and wonder. Here is the epitome of a man at ease with the long, large view of existence.

Appropriately enough, a model of his "laboratory" is spread out at his feet—a map of the universe—a twenty-eight-foot field of granite in which 2,700 small metal studs are embedded. These represent the relative location of the planets, sixth-magnitude stars, and other celestial objects as they were at noon on April 22, 1979, when the memorial was dedicated.

The statue is remarkably well placed with regard to other powerful places.

Just behind Einstein's statue is the National Academy of Sciences Building. To the east rises the white obelisk of the Washington Monument, and farther on the Capitol Building of the United States of America.

South, across a grassy field, the shiny black granite of the Vietnam Memorial is cut into the earth.

Over to the right, the grave face of Abraham Lincoln looks out from his marble rotunda.

And across the Potomac River, the flame that burns on John Kennedy's grave is visible in the early evening.

Each time I visit Washington, I come here to sit for a time on Einstein's lap and think. His demeanor is inviting. His knee accommodating. With so many reminders of the human enterprise visible in all directions, Einstein's knee becomes an intersection where powerful forces meet—those arising from the complicated human capacity for pain and sorrow, promise and glory, wonder and awe.

More than anything, Einstein wished to reveal the single common law governing the universe. To state in one ultimate simple equation the unifying property of space, time, matter, energy, gravitation, and electromagnetism. He was in quest of a unified field theory. He failed in this quest.

An unresolvable polarity resisted his genius.

* * *

Einstein worked his equations in the invisible, abstract world of quantum physics. His conclusions there coincide with the experience of daily existence. He lived, as we live, in the bipolar world of wet and dry, love and hate, peace and war, hard and soft, light and dark, yes and no.

SHE WAS CALLED "LOVEY." REAL NAME—TRUE story. She taught me how to swear and dip snuff, how to sing the blues and iron shirts. Five days a week she did the housework and cooking for my family. My mother worked in the family business during the years I was in high school. When I came home each afternoon, Lovey was there to look after me. And there to continue my education in subjects not taught in school.

She was young, perhaps thirty-five, with fine features, curly black hair, and light brown skin. Neat and precise in her habits. Strong and clear in her opinions. Unmarried, she took care of her blind father, who played guitar and sang on the downtown streets, with a tin cup on the sidewalk in front of him.

Lovey didn't fit the cultural stereotype of the hymn-singing, humble mammy. Maybe my mother thought of her that way, but behind my mother's back Lovey mimicked her, sang raunchy songs, dipped snuff, bad-mouthed white folks, and used all the foul language a rebellious teenager like me so admired. My mother thought of Lovey as my baby-sitter, but Lovey was in truth the high priestess in charge of the rituals of my coming of age, and thereby one of the most influential people in my life—then and now.

One day she handed me her snuff can. Said she knew I was just waiting for a chance to get into it when she wasn't looking, so I might as well learn how to dip snuff right.

First get a little twig from the yard and chew the end soft and wet. Then dip the twig into the snuff and put the end of the twig under your tongue and suck on it.

After about three dip-and-sucks, I got sick and dizzy and had to lie down for a while. My respect for Lovey went up, since she could handle strong tobacco and I couldn't. But thanks to her, I could boast to my peers, "Sure, hell yes, I've used snuff."

For the same reason, she gave me my first drink of homemade corn liquor. With similar results. For the rest of my life, I left snuff and corn liquor alone.

* * *

When my mother wasn't around, Lovey sang the blues. I didn't know it was the blues at the time. I just thought it was what Lovey sang. She didn't sing about Jesus or heaven or sweet chariots. Her singing was about getting up in the morning and dealing with the day. About love and sex and sorrow. About disappointment and not having any money and the roof leaking and jelly rolls and catching the next train for Chicago and finding some man better than the one who never came around anymore anyway.

I could relate. Oh, could I relate. I was an adolescent. Undersized, oversexed, ugly, skinny, pimply, and lonely. In need of cash, a good time, and a good woman, along with better grades and my own car.

Sing them blues.

About the same time that orthodontia, hormones, genes, a burr haircut with ducktails, and a '37 Chevrolet improved my self-image, Lovey announced to me that it was time for me to learn to iron my own shirts.

I had no idea what was involved in ironing a shirt, because Lovey ironed alone. Always in the best room of the house—the dining room—where there was lots of light and a good view down the street. Sometimes when I got home from school, she'd just be finishing up—always in a good mood then—singing and talking and laughing to herself.

But my respect for Lovey was such that if ironing was good enough for her, it was good enough for me.

Here's what I learned.

First, you have to start with good shirts—all heavy white cotton—or you're wasting your time. Be sure to check the pockets, and shake the shirt to get rid of any lint or loose dirt. Check the buttons to make sure they're all there in good shape. Then you've got to wash right. Wash whites separately— never wash coloreds and whites together. Use a tiny bit of bleach and bluing and starch, so the shirts come out the color of frosted ice. Hang the shirts outside in the sunshine until they are not quite dry. Wrap them in a clean white damp dish-towel and put them in the refrigerator.

Next, set up your ironing board, making sure the cover is clean and tight, then put it in a right place—where you like to be—where you feel good. Get a cola bottle with a sprinkling head on it and fill the bottle with cold water. Get some hangers. Get your iron—a big, heavy iron—and make sure the bottom is clean. Plug the iron in and set the heat at high. Sit a spell, have a cup of coffee. Don't hurry.

Get one shirt at a time out of the refrigerator. Understand from the beginning that you're going to iron around the shirt three times. The first time is to smooth wrinkles and "set" the shirt. Sprinkle a little water this time on any place that's not damp. The second time around is to press the shirt dry and sharp. The third time is to tidy the little places and finish the collar and cuffs real stiff.

Each time, you go around in this order: cuffs (both sides), sleeves, collar (both sides, backside first, ironing away from the points), then the front placket (back side first, top to bottom, stretching the fabric), then all the way around from front to back, then carefully around the buttons.

Do it all over again, get the shoulders and high back yoke this time really carefully, the mark of a professional. Make sure the shirt is crisp dry.

The last time around, you just check to see that you haven't missed a single wrinkle and that the cuffs and collar are perfectly smooth. Even the finest workman needs to inspect his work critically.

Carefully, now, you place the shirt on a hanger—button just the top button. Finally, you hang it out in the sunshine to give it a fresh smell. When you've done one shirt, sit down, take a little break, have some snuff.

Never, never hurry—you'll scorch the shirt and scorch your soul.

When I complained that this was sure a lot of trouble to go to over a shirt, Lovey explained: "You'll never regret knowing how to do at least one thing exactly right, and if you don't do it right the first time, when will you find time to go back and do it over?"

It took Lovey about the same amount of time to iron a shirt as it has taken me to explain her style—she didn't rush, but she was efficient. It took me most of an afternoon to iron one shirt. Even then I scorched the collar. But after a while, I got the hang of it. It was a proud moment when Lovey inspected a shirt I had ironed and said it wasn't bad for a white boy.

And Lovey was right—whatever success or failure I've had at whatever else I've tried to do, in my heart I hold this rock-solid fact: At least I can iron a shirt right. A shirt that could be put in the shirt-ironing hall of fame.

In 1972 I went to Japan to live in a Buddhist monastery—to seek spiritual enlightenment. Unable to accommodate myself to the austere discipline of silent, sitting meditation, I was introduced to active meditation. Practiced alone and silently, this involved doing mundane tasks in a deliberate fashion so as to focus the mind. As the teacher explained, "Given careful attention, any activity may become a window on the universe and a doorway to understanding."

While raking the gravel paths in the monastery garden, I had an "oh, of course" experience. I realized I knew about this. This wasn't Buddhism. It was Loveyism. Raking a gravel path right was just like ironing a shirt right.

As has been the case so often in my life, I had

gone to a great deal of trouble and expense to find out something I already knew.

I recall the details of ironing a shirt because that's still the way I do it.

To this day, I usually tend my own shirts.

Only because it gives me solitary pleasure.

The kind we all enjoy alone when doing our nails or taking a bath or shaving or weeding in the garden or chopping wood or knitting or baking bread or hanging sheets out on a clothesline.

Sure, sometimes these activities are just a matter of taking care of personal business or routine tasks. But as often as not, we use these times to reflect and talk to ourselves.

Or meditate—even pray.

Just because you aren't on your knees in church or sitting still in a cramped position doesn't mean you can't be talking to God. Just because both you and God are busy doesn't mean you can't be in touch.

Such times are the sacred part of the secret life.

Such times keep my soul sane.

When I asked my mother difficult questions, she would avoid complicated explanations by saying, "Someday you'll understand." Lovey taught me that while I was waiting for some understanding to come, I could iron a shirt.

31

WHILE I WAS FILLING OUT A FORM THIS WEEK, I wondered how many times in my life I have written down my name, place of birth, and address. It seems like such simple information, yet it has complications.

NAME: _____

The first blank on your birth certificate and every other form and application you'll see for the rest of your life. However, "What's your name?" and "What do people call you?" are questions with shifting answers.

My parents chose "Robert Edward Lee Fulghum" because my daddy was a Civil War buff and admired the general. But the registrar of births could only handle three names. My folks settled for "Robert Lee Fulghum." When I asked them, "Why Robert?" they couldn't remember.

"Bobby Lee," was what my parents usually called me.

"Sonny boy." My dad called me that, child and man, all his life. The day I went off to first grade and the evening I caught the train for college, and the night of my wedding and the day of the birth of my first child, it was the same: "Good luck, sonny boy."

"Beaver Bob." By my running mates in the "Jolly Boys Club" in junior high—before the orthodontist had a go at my teeth.

"Goodtime Bobby Fulghum." After orthodontia, in high school.

"Number 36." My lucky number when I was in rodeos.

"Big Bunny." By Marilyn, my first love. Think what you want.

"Fulghy." In college, and even now by men friends at poker games.

"Daddy." Children.

"Ensign Fulghum." As a navy chaplain trainee.

"The Reverend Mr. Fulghum." After ordination.

"Uncle Bob." By my art students.

"Ano Ne." Second wife. (Japanese familiar for "Hey, you.")

"Zulu Delta Ground." Radio code name when I was ground crew at a glider contest.

"Captain Kindergarten." After the book, by acquaintances.

"Dr. Feelgood." How the critics refer to me sometimes.

"Dear." As in "Dear Mr. Fulghum." Also by my wife, on tense days, as in "Are you going to walk through here again with muddy feet, *dear*?"

"Granddaddy" and "Poppa." By Sarah, Max, and Brie.

"Robert-Not-Bob." What I used to tell people my name was, but it never worked. They'd just say, "Well, sure, Bob, whatever you want."

There are even more—about thirty names in all, but that's enough to make the point. All of these are names given me by other people. But not names I would have given myself. My name is not mine, it's theirs. It's a series of costumes put on my life by other people.

I remember reading in some anthropology book about cultures in which your original name is given you by your family until you are old enough to choose a name for yourself. I would have liked that.

In high school, I wanted to be called "Doak" or "Buck" or "Ace."

Later, when I was in seminary in Berkeley, I went to foreign movies and always stayed for the credits at the end to see if I could find some elegant, mysterious, strong name from another country that I could use. "Miloslav" or "Czabt" or "Jean-Pierre."

In the sixties, when the hippies reached for more expressive names and I considered myself at least semi-hip, I briefly considered "Nigel Seven Morningstar" as a name tag connecting me to the Age of Aquarius.

But now I guess it's too late or too much trouble. The name is not that important anymore—it's the tone that counts. I feel like an old dog I know. He will come to any name you call him, just so long as your demeanor carries with it the promise of affection or food.

An actor I met in Roanoke, Virginia, solved a name problem for me. He's my age and has grandchildren. We talked about the hidden disappointment of names that get stuck on you when your children have children. This happens at a time when you have reached seniority in the ranks. You feel experienced and wise. Some respect is due. You deserve it. And then some slobbering little bundle of joy who can't speak the language starts calling you "Boppa" or "Nungnung" or "Moomaw."

And everybody thinks it's so damned cute. Not only does the child call you that, but everybody else in the family starts calling you that. There's nothing you can do about it. You feel for sure like the old family dog.

How can you have a dignified role in the life of the family when everybody thinks of you as good old "Moomaw" or "Gandy Bippy"?

But this guy I met in Roanoke beat the system. Actually, his wife had the idea.

Her name was plain old "Mary." She hated it all her life. She saw this "Gandy Bippy" thing coming and was determined to head it off. When her first grandchild reached the age of semiconscious intelligence, she carefully explained to the child that Grandmother was to be called "Delilah" and nothing else. "Delilah"—after that sexpot in the Bible who did a number on old Samson.

Her husband didn't much care to be called "Samson," but since he had been "Fred" all his life and didn't much care for that either, he opted for the German nickname "Fritz." He's not German, but "Fritz" had a certain lively, foreign sound.

It took the family a while to get used to the fact that Granny and Grandpa were usually unavailable for child-care duty. However, Delilah and Fritz would be glad to take the children to the zoo or anywhere else, anytime, just call their names.

PLACE OF BIRTH: _____

How many times have you filled in that blank? All our official records bear it. Our obituaries will carry it. "Where were you born?" The question always comes up.

And from me always gets a reply of "It's not really very important." My family and I lived there about six weeks and have never returned.

Ask me instead where I spent my childhood, where I spent those years of grade school and junior high school and high school. Ask me what it was like one mile in any direction from my house at age nine. Ask me where I grew up. Ask me, "Where do you come from?"

There's yet another question in this vein—one

never asked in official forms. It exists only in the secret biographical records of my mind.

CONCEPTION: _____

Where was I conceived—and under what circumstances?

Since both my parents are dead, I'll never know. But I'd like to know. I'd *really* like to know.

They spent the years I can remember sleeping in separate beds in separate rooms. Never once did I see them embrace or kiss one another. At times they fought, but most of the time they were politely civil. They led lives apart.

I wonder how was it for them at the beginning. How were they feeling when I was conceived? As best I can figure, it must have been in early September. Where? Was it planned or an accident? A matter of love and passion or a matter of course? Was I wanted? Did they at least love each other then?

For reasons I cannot articulate, it would settle my mind to know.

Over the last year, I've asked many people these two questions: "Where were you conceived?" or "Where were your children conceived?"

A surprising number of people seem to have come into being as a consequence of passion and laughter. Not a bad mix for a beginning. Sites and occasions that stand out so far in my poll: in an elevator, on a windowsill, in a boat, in a closet, in the backseat of a car, in an outhouse, in a bathroom during a reception after a funeral, in a church office, in an airplane, and in front of the TV while watching Nixon make a speech.

A young friend told me what she knew about her conception and birth.

For reasons she will never comprehend, she was placed for adoption the week she was born, even though her parents were married at the time. Years later, when she was thirty, she was reunited with her biological parents. She asked many questions, especially about the "why" of the adoption. The answers were difficult and confusing to her, because her biological parents were equally confused about it—then, and now.

Her father told her it might make some difference to her to know that when she was conceived, he was in love with her mother and she with him; that they were engaged to be married in late summer. They were young—not yet twenty-one. It was April. And that on a lovely, warm Saturday afternoon in the spring in Texas, they went on a hike along a remote and secluded section of a river. They waded in the water, played, splashed one another until they were soaking wet. They took their clothes off and made love in great passion, in the

41

hot sunshine, on a sandbank in the middle of the river. The Spanish had named that river *"Los Brazos de Dios"*—the arms of God.

In a way, this story answers the question of my own conception.

Wherever and however any one of us may be conceived, it is the same.

We come into being in the arms of God.

A FTER THE BLANKS FOR NAME AND PLACE OF birth on official forms, we come to

ADDRESS: _____

Where do you live? For many of us, the answer changes often in a lifetime.

Nearly one in five Americans moves every year. About half the population has moved in the past five years, according to the most recent census. More than 19 million people will move between Memorial Day and Labor Day this year.

Not surprising. We've always been a nation of migrants. We think the earliest arrivals came across a land bridge from Asia, and 65 million more people sailed from Europe to North America between the seventeenth century and the Second World War. Even after we got to the edge of this continent, we kept on moving.

The genealogists in my clan say I can follow my own genes by starting with a Danish sea raider, who rowed off to what became Normandy in the eighth century. From there the gene strain invaded England, Virginia, North Carolina, Tennessee, Texas, and Washington State.

Still there's no settling down. I've moved my domicile twenty-seven times in fifty-five years. And that's not counting short-term addresses connected to college dorms, summer jobs, and military training.

I moved again this year.

Here's my change-of-address notice:

I have been living aboard a houseboat in Seattle. Now, for part of the year I live in another neighborhood—San Juan County, Utah.

You may not realize it, but you've seen this Utah landscape. It's high desert, red-rock canyon-lands country. John Wayne filmed some of his most famous cowboy pictures hereabouts. And every now and then, there is an ad on TV showing a beautiful woman in an evening gown marooned alone with a late-model pickup truck on top of a thousand-foot sandstone spire out in the middle of nowhere. These places are in my new neighborhood.

I've never figured out how that ad would make me want to buy a truck, but I do know why I would want to spend time in a place that seems so open and empty and far from civilization. *Because* it is open and empty and seems so far from civilization.

My wife and I lived in a small house in this landscape last year. Twenty miles from town. No telephone, no television or radio, no newspaper delivery. The daily news is what time the sun comes up and the phases of the moon, whether or not there is firewood, and the effect the seasons have on living things, including me.

If you fly over it, the landscape seems rugged, dry, and barren. Not so. Its best parts are just spread out over time and space. You have to look. Within an hour of my house, I've stood in dinosaur tracks more than 140 million years old and picked pine nuts for lunch; watched wild horses run and slept in an Indian ruin abandoned nine hundred years ago. I've been where it was so quiet and still I could hear the sounds made by the wings of ravens as they flew overhead.

It's not as remote as I had expected. Maybe nowhere is remote anymore. The interstate highway is thirty miles away. In the nearest little town, most people have satellite-TV dishes that pull in more stations than you'd get in a city. *USA Today* is on the newsstands early every morning. UPS and Federal Express deliver "second day." And the kids in the local high school look and dress and think like their peers in Seattle or L.A.

There's been a lot of human traffic through this countryside. At one time or another, during the last thousand years, the culture of the area has been shaped by Anasazi, Ute, and Navajo Indians, Spanish explorers, Mormon settlers, cattle ranchers, sheepherders, pinto-bean farmers, uranium miners, mountain bikers, river runners, Jeepers, big-game hunters, and drive-through tourists. Everybody passing through leaves a mark.

It's not paradise. The once-charming little centers of civilization have died off or become motel strips. The weather contrasts are extreme. Drought and downpour, 105 degrees in August and 10 below in January. A week of dust storm followed by a week of icy gale is not uncommon. It's not hard to die of thirst if you get lost in the back country. The fear of rattlesnakes, black-widow spiders, scorpions, and biting flies is barely counterbalanced by the anticipation of wildflowers in spring and aspen trees in the fall.

Still, I like it. Something is there that sustains my spirit and lifts me up.

It's a matter of locale. I think everybody resonates to some specific landscape. I grew up in open country—hot and dry country—and spent the happiest days of my early life on horseback as a working cowboy and dude wrangler. I have photographs of my father and his father and his father and his father—all on horseback in work clothes.

I'm not a cowboy now—don't pretend to be, but I am most at ease in that raw country and feel comfortable in my own skin when I'm surrounded by that rough environment. It's where I go when I get confused. It's enough just to be for a while in a place where all I can hear is the wind blowing, and all I can see is a long way off in the distance on the earth around me in the daytime and a long way off in the distance in the night sky above me. It is there and then I know I am not lost.

A TELEPHONE CALL LAST OCTOBER. "MR. FUL-ghum, our first-grade class would like to involve you in a field trip." It's the chairlady of the Outside Education Committee for the first-grade class in the only elementary school in our small nearby town in Utah.

A field trip! Yes! Talk about magic words! Next to Show-and-Tell, I liked field trips best when I was in school. Actually, I'd been thinking about field trips quite recently. About a month before receiving this invitation, I stood on the sidewalk of the town and watched with envy as a fire truck rolled by very slowly with its sirens wailing. This was to please the first-graders who were sitting in back on top of the hoses, holding on for dear life, grinning from ear to ear, thrilled beyond words by a trip down Main Street with the firemen. A small voice in the back of my head said, "Take me, too."

I remember with astonishing clarity my own field-trip experiences of fifty years ago. To a fire station, a bakery, the Coca-Cola bottling plant, a dairy, the police station, the city dump, and a construction site. During second grade, we visited an automobile-repair garage, rode a city bus around and back to the place where the bus was kept at night, and toured the county museum. We walked up and down our main street going in and out of businesses to see what was going on behind the scenes where groceries and goods were being unloaded and unpacked. And, of course, the zoo—we went to the zoo several times. And when the circus came to town, we were there to watch them unload the animals from the train and set up the tent.

Looking at a book in a classroom could not ever compete with a field trip.

How sorry I was when education shifted to matters that could only be studied in school in the classroom. How glad I was to take geology in college and go out on field trips again—to walk on and touch what I was studying.

When my children were young and the call came from school for parent volunteers to chaperon field trips, I was their man. Once a field-trip project involved building a fifteen-foot-high hot-air balloon out of paper—then flying it at a nearby park. The balloon caught fire up in the air and floated toward a landing on the roof of a nearby house. The fire department was called. Very exciting! When calm had been restored, the students wanted to do it again. Not just the balloon, but the whole catastrophe, launch, flaming balloon, fire department, and all.

When I became a schoolteacher myself, of drawing and writing and philosophy, I learned to drive a school bus so I could take my students on field trips. At the heart of my drawing class was the notion that an artist begins by looking carefully at the real world. An artist never looks away or turns away. An artist's job is to see. And to go out in the world and see it firsthand, just as it is; to report with line and words what is seen. To be *in* the world, not just study *about* the world, that is the artist's task. So we got in the bus and sallied forth.

Even as a parish minister, I held to this notion. When I was in seminary, I read about something called the French Catholic Worker-Priest Movement. These men had regular jobs during the week like everyone else—plumber, electrician, teacher— any useful job at all. On the weekends, they celebrated mass. They chose to be part of the world, not just work in the church.

I decided to follow their example. During the years I was a parish minister, I usually had a full-time weekday job like everybody else. I had to be at work on Monday at seven-thirty. I made a clear choice. One could concentrate on being *in the world*, or one could spend time mostly *in the church*. One could address the world or one could do church workwork.

Only now have I finally realized that my life has been an unending field trip.

And I have tried hard not to be a tourist.

But to be an adventurer, a traveler, an explorer, a learner, and a pilgrim.

So you can understand my enthusiasm when I was asked if I would like to be involved in a first-grade field trip. This is not kid stuff. "Of course! Wonderful! Where are we going to go?"

"Oh, I'm sorry, Mr. Fulghum, I guess I didn't make myself clear. We want to come see you. You are our field trip."

I didn't know what to say.

The ultimate turn of the wheel of life, I guess.

I have *become* a field trip.

"Well," I sighed, "come on over—my zoo is open."

*I*N 1991, TWO HIKERS FOUND THE MUMMIFIED BODY of a man in the melting ice of a glacier on the Swiss-Italian border. The early scientific studies indicated the man had lived and died 5,300 years ago. In the Bronze Age.

Out of all the fascinating conclusions reached by the examiners, one in particular lodged in my mind: The man's hair showed clear evidence of having been deliberately shortened.

In whatever passed for a Bronze Age barbershop, our man had a haircut.

I read about this in the newspaper while sitting in a barber's chair getting my own hair trimmed. Looking at the sketch of the "ice man" and looking at the crew sitting around in chairs waiting their turn, I figured if this ancient one walked in and sat down, nobody would pay him that much attention. He'd fit right in with the crowd that hangs out in my barbershop.

Weekly, I go for a haircut. Not because I'm that concerned with tonsorial tidiness. I have a fondness for small-town barbershops and the tale-tellers who hang out in them. Old guys who fought and still fight the Great Wars, but who spend a lot of time discussing prostate problems and the new nurse over at the clinic. A relative newcomer like me is fair game for the tales they've told a hundred times. Here's one told on a Saturday afternoon in October. Have a seat.

Our storyteller is best described by his cousin as "barbed-wire lean and barbed-wire mean—he chews nails and spits rust." A flinty little old man with a plank-flat face weathered ruddy brown below a line just over his eyebrows. Above that line his face is pasty white from a lifetime of wearing a hat. Add to his two-tone face a nose red-veined from too much hard drinking, plus some curly tufts of hair on the side of his bald head, and you have a joker's face without benefit of greasepaint. It's hard to believe he was once the town mortician and a deputy sheriff. He's eighty-two now and occupies his time being the resident historian at the barbershop called Moon's.

"Moon's Barbershop. Used to belong to old Moon McCloud. That's where this place got its name, you know, from him. He run the best barbershop this town ever seen. They called him 'Moon' because of what he did in the Big War. Got himself captured over in France and them Germans they hauled him off to a prisoner-of-war camp. Well, he got fed up with them krauts who ran the camp and one day at a count-up when his number was called he turned around and mooned 'em—dropped his pants and hung his behind out at 'em. One of them krauts shot him in the butt right there. Bam. Wrecked his ass all right, but it made him a hero. The other prisoners called him 'General Moon' after that. Give him a medal made out of tinfoil—for bravery beyond the call of duty. A little hard to explain when he got home, but word got around and people was always asking him to drop his pants so they could see his war wounds. Moon he wouldn't do it. But he was elected commander of the American Legion on account of what he done. A hero. Only one we had.

"Well, old Moon he opened himself this barbershop in the back end of his daddy's old service station. Learned to cut hair in the prisoner camp. He hated being a barber, but he said it was a job he could do standing up, since he had half his butt missing and sitting down was hard. He only had one price and one kind of haircut—cheap and guaranteed to be shorter when you left than when you come in.

"Moon he was ambitious. He ran the service station and the barber shop and got himself appointed to be a justice of the peace and a notary public, too. When the uranium boom come to town, old Moon he added a little café and grocery store to the barbershop. Said he was going to be the first stand-up millionaire in the world. You could get just about anything you wanted over at Moon's—haircut, get married, eat lunch, tank of gas, six-pack and a quart of milk, loaf of bread, and drive off. We always said all he needed was some hardware up front and a whorehouse out back, and he'd have all the bases covered.

"But Moon he died before he was sixty. Right in the middle of collecting the offering in the Methodist church one Sunday morning. His heart attacked him. Preacher said Jesus took him. Hard to believe Jesus needed a barber. Don't ask me. Don't know nothing about religion. All I remember is Moon saying he didn't care where he went after he died just as long as he could sit down in comfort forever after. A lifetime is a long time to stand."

*I*T'S FEBRUARY. MORNING. COLD, GRAY, WINDY, wet.

Winter conditions outside and inside. A morning to crawl back into bed, pull up the covers, and wait for something better to happen. Like spring, for instance. Instead, I am in a doctor's waiting room in a small-town hospital. In a state of nonspecific ill health. Miserable in body, soul, and mind. Don't know why. "You're going in for a checkup," says my wife. So here I am. Fix me.

Across from me is an aged couple, sitting side by side, holding hands.

Neat and clean, washed and pressed. In her white hair, the woman wears a flowery arrangement—holly with red berries and some red poinsettia leaves. Odd.

The old man catches my eye, breaks into a grin, and says, "Merry Christmas!" My automatic pilot shoves "Merry Christmas!" out of my mouth at the same time that my brain wakes up and asks, "What, what, what . . . ?"

The old man sings softly: "Oh, you better watch out, you better not cry, you better not pout, I'm telling you why: Santa Claus is coming to town." He finishes the song, chuckles to himself, and again addresses me with a cheerful "Merry Christmas!" His wife smiles.

Just then the nurse sings out from behind her desk, "Merry Christmas, Uncle Ed. The doctor will see you now." From down the hall, the doctor shouts, "Merry Christmas, Ed! Good to see you."

(Right. Maybe it's me. Maybe it really is December instead of February. Mind is going. I knew this would happen someday. Why now?)

The nurse and the old man pass down the hall to an examination room.

Uncle Ed's wife crosses over to sit by me. A bit embarrassed, she apologizes, pats me on the knee, and explains:

"I hope he didn't upset you. The doctor says he's had a minor stroke or two and may be in the beginning stages of Alzheimer's. But in our family we know it's just that he's getting old and feeble. He's eighty-eight, and his wiring's coming loose. Most of the time he's OK, but every once in a while something a little crazy happens. Like this Christmas thing. A couple of years ago he shouted down from upstairs something about how he'd forgotten it was Christmas Eve and hadn't we better get the ornaments out and the packages wrapped. I didn't know what to think. Because it was March. But we didn't have anything else to do that day, and I thought I might as well humor him. So we spent the morning getting ready for Christmas. I called the girls—we have three grown daughters—and they came over for lunch and helped untangle the lights and wrap some packages. We sang carols and made cookies and had a wonderful time.

"When the girls left, he asked me to tell him about Christmas when he was a boy—because he was having a hard time remembering. Now I've known this man all my life. He had a terrible childhood, father was a drunk—beat him and his mother all the time. His father ran off with a woman from the drugstore, and his mother took sick and stayed home in bed most of the time. Ed never had a Christmas when he was a child. Well, how could I bring all that up again? I just didn't have the heart.

"We've been married sixty years. And I've never lied to him, ever. But I decided I'd just make up some good memories for him. What harm would it do? So I told him about the year he got a tricycle, and the year there was a wind-up train under the tree, and the year he saw Santa Claus, and the year he got to be in the Christmas pageant at church. It made him very happy—me remembering the Christmases he never had but always wanted.

"You know, we never did get around to Christmas that March. Just Christmas Eve. Because by evening his mind was back in the present. Christmas Eve and good memories seemed to be enough.

"But four months later it happened all over again. I heard him singing carols upstairs one morning, and here came Christmas down the stairs. MERRY CHRISTMAS! Again in July. Also in October—instead of Halloween. Twice in December. And now in February.

"Every time, he wants me to tell him about his childhood again, and I do. I'm getting so good at lying about how wonderful his Christmas used to be that I half believe it myself. I call the girls each time, and they come over to help out. They're really into it now. They bring him presents and sing carols and bake cookies. And twice we've even got as far as putting up a tree. They love to do it. See, they don't think of it as Christmas anymore. They think of it as Father's Day."

* * *

Just then the old man comes shuffling back up the hall. He and the nurse are finishing off a last chorus of "Jingle Bells." They both shout "Merry Christmas!" at me, and I shout "Merry Christmas!" right back at them.

The old lady patted my knee again, smiled, and rose to leave with her husband. He gallantly held the door open for her, and they went off into another day, hand in hand.

I didn't have time to ask her what they did when other holidays came up.

But I guess every day is Valentine's Day for them.

*T*HAT OLD LADY IN THE VALENTINE STORY PLANTED a seed in my head that didn't sprout until the following November. She had said, "It's kind of refreshing to have Christmas come as a surprise."

The early warning signs of the inevitable coming of the holiday juggernaut had appeared in the form of gift catalogs in late September. A fog of anxious dread began rising out of my spiritual swamp. By November I was in a serious Christmas-phobia funk. I wanted out. I lay awake half a night with a full committee meeting going on in my head. In the morning, I wrote a letter.

Dear Family and Friends:
I saw the cover of the December issue of *Esquire* magazine this week and bought it to take

home to my wife. Because the headline on the cover fitted my mood exactly:

"O H M Y G O D (It's Christmas)"

Maybe "Jeezus Christ, here comes Christmas again" would be more ironically accurate. Neither exclamation reflects much joy.

Nevertheless, Lynn and I couldn't seem to help falling into the inevitable what-are-we-going-to-do-about-Christmas discussion—the exasperating one that leads to deep sighs and the making of long lists of people and long lists of things to buy and long lists of things to do as soon as possible even though soon is not so possible. Christmas as a crisis.

At about the same time, we both realized we are just not into doing the Christmas thing this year—at least not in the usual way. It's not that we've become Scroogish about the season—it's that we don't want to become Scroogish.

We are still influenced by the memory of being in New Mexico for part of the holiday season last year. We passed through the manic little tourist town of Taos, which was geared up for the maximum level of kitschy consumerism, and drove farther on up the road to the Taos Indian pueblo.

Peace and quiet reigned there. The time from December 15 to January 15 is observed as "The time of being still." The pueblo is closed to tourists and all commercial activity for a month. To us it felt like the little town of Bethlehem must have been a long time ago.

And so, in the sensible spirit of our Indian cousins, we intend being still this year. We're not going shopping. The money we might have spent can go to some other good cause. Take the time you might have spent shopping for us and be still a little yourself. Think of us, who wish you quiet joy this Christmas. God rest you, merry gentlemen, and gentlewomen, too—God rest you.

In late December, my wife and I went off to Utah for a time—just the two of us. On Christmas Eve we chopped up the trunk of last year's tree and built a fire to sit by while we ate homemade bread and chili. We took a long walk up the valley in the snow.

We came upon a midnight clear.

The silent stars went by.

The world in solemn stillness lay.

And when the angels sang, we were there to hear them.

*T*HAT EXPERIMENT IN CHRISTMAS DAMAGE CONTROL has continued and expanded.

Since Christmas went so well, I explained to my family and friends that I would like to try treating other official occasions in a similar way. I asked them to forgive me my obligations for birthdays or anniversaries for a while. And I would do the same for them—no expectations.

I wanted to be free of dates. How would it be, I wondered, to celebrate the seasons of the heart as opportunities, not obligations? I promised to keep them in the forefront of my thinking—all those whom I love and cherish. I promised to pay attention to them and give to them when they most need something but least expect it. To let gifts and favors and affirmations come, from me, as a surprise.

How's it going? As I write, it's February, and I'm thirteen months into the trial. It hasn't been easy. It means getting funny looks when official dates are imminent. It takes extra effort, but the effort so far is pleasure, not hassle. Friends and family seem to like knowing I'm thinking about them, but it's hard to tell enthusiasm from friendly toleration sometimes. Only my five-year-old granddaughter has actually complained. She would like to be surprised a little more regularly.

I don't know what my friends and family really think about this experiment in gift-giving. They don't say, and I haven't asked. They are all ahead in actual loot, if one looks at this deal from a strict accounting point of view. But that's not the point.

The heart will turn to a prune if love is always by the numbers.

How will you know someone really loves you if they only meet your expectations and not your needs?

A MAN AND WOMAN I KNOW FELL INTO BIG LOVE somewhat later in life than usual. She was forty. He was fifty. Neither had been married before. But they knew about marriage. They had seen the realities of that sacred state up close among their friends. They determined to overcome as many potential difficulties as possible by working things out in advance.

Prenuptial agreements over money and property were prepared by lawyers. Preemptive counseling over perceived tensions was provided by a psychologist, who helped them commit all practical promises to paper, with full reciprocal tolerance for irrational idiosyncrasies.

"Get married once, do it right, and live at least agreeably, if not happily, ever after." So they hoped.

One item in their agreement concerned pets and kids. Item Number 7:

"We agree to have either children or pets, but not both."

The man was not enthusiastic about dependent relationships. Kids, dogs, cats, hamsters, goldfish, snakes, or any other living thing that had to be fed or watered had never had a place in his life. Not even houseplants. And especially not dogs. She, on the other hand, liked taking care of living things. Especially children and dogs.

OK. But she had to choose. She chose children. He obliged. Two daughters in three years. Marriage and family life went along quite well for all. Their friends were impressed. So far, so good.

The children reached school age. The mother leapt eagerly into the bottomless pool of educational volunteerism. The school needed funds for art and music. The mother organized a major-league auction to raise much money. Every family agreed to provide an item of substantial value for the event.

The mother knew a lot about dogs. She had raised dogs all her life—the pedigreed champion kind. She planned to use her expertise to shop the various local puppy pounds to find an unnoticed bargain pooch and shape it up for the auction as her contribution. With a small investment, she would make a tenfold profit for the school. And for a couple of days, at least, there would be a dog in the house.

After a month of looking, she found the wonder dog—the dog of great promise. Female, four months old, dark gray, blue eyes, tall, strong, confident, and very, very, *very* friendly.

To her practiced eye, our mother could see that classy genes had been accidentally mixed here. Two purebred dogs of the highest caliber had combined to produce this exceptional animal. Most likely a black Labrador and a weimaraner, she thought. Perfect. Just perfect.

To those of us of untutored eye, this mutt looked more like the results of a bad blind date between a Mexican burro and a miniature musk-ox.

The fairy dogmother went to work. Dog is inspected and given shots by a vet. Fitted with an elegant leather collar and leash. Equipped with a handsome bowl, a ball, and a rawhide bone. Expenses: $50 to the pound, $50 to the vet, $50 to the beauty parlor, $60 for tack and equipment, and $50 for food. A total of $260 on a dog that is going to stay forty-eight hours before auction time.

The father took one look and paled. He smelled smoke. He wouldn't give ten bucks to keep it an hour. "DOG," as the father named it, has a long, thick rubber club of a tail, legs and feet that remind him of hairy toilet plungers, and is already big enough at four months to bowl over the girls and their mother with its unrestrained enthusiasm.

The father knows this is going to be ONE BIG

DOG. Something a zoo might display. Omnivorous, it has eaten all its food in one day and has left permanent teeth marks on a chair leg, a leather ottoman, and the father's favorite golf shoes.

The father is patient about all of this.

After all, it is only a temporary arrangement, and for a good cause.

He remembers item No. 7 in the prenuptial agreement.

He is safe.

On Thursday night, the school affair gets off to a winning start. Big crowd of parents, and many guests who look flush with money. Arty decorations, fine potluck food, a cornucopia of auction items. The mother basks in her triumph.

"DOG" comes on the auction block much earlier than planned. Because the father went out to the car to check on "DOG" and found it methodically eating the leather off the car's steering wheel, after having crunched holes in the padded dashboard.

After a little wrestling match getting "DOG" into the mother's arms and up onto the stage, the mother sits in a folding chair, cradling "DOG" with the solemn tenderness reserved for a corpse at a wake, while the auctioneer describes the pedigree of the animal and all the fine effort and neat equipment thrown in with the deal.

"What am I bid for this wonderful animal?"

"A hundred dollars over here; two hundred dollars on the right; two hundred and fifty dollars in the middle."

There is a sniffle from the mother.

Tears are running down her face.

"DOG" is licking the tears off her cheeks.

In a whisper not really meant for public notice, the mother calls to her husband: *"Jack, Jack, I can't sell this dog—I want this dog—this is my dog—she loves me—I love her—oh, Jack."*

Every eye in the room is on this soapy drama.

The father feels ill, realizing that the great bowling ball of fate is headed down his alley.

"Please, Jack, please, please," she whispers.

At that moment, everybody in the room knows who is going to buy the pooch. "DOG" is going home with Jack.

Having no fear now of being stuck themselves, several relieved men set the bidding on fire. "DOG" is going to set an auction record. The repeated hundred-dollar rise in price is matched by the soft *"Please, Jack"* from the stage and Jack's almost inaudible raise in the bidding, five dollars at a time.

There is a long pause at "Fifteen hundred dollars—going once, going twice ..."

A sob from the stage.

And for $1,505 Jack has bought himself a dog.

Add in the up-front costs, and he's $1,765 into "DOG."

The noble father is applauded as his wife rushes from the stage to throw her arms around his neck, while "DOG" wraps the leash around both their legs and down they go into the first row of chairs. A memorable night for the PTA.

I see Jack out being walked by the dog late at night. He's the only one strong enough to control it, and he hates to have the neighbors see him being dragged along by this, the most expensive damned dog for a hundred miles.

"DOG" has become "Marilyn." She is big enough to plow with now. "Marilyn" may be the world's dumbest dog, having been to obedience school twice with no apparent effect.

Jack is still stunned. He can't believe this has happened to him.

He had it down on paper. No. 7. Kids or pets, not both.

But the complicating clauses in the fine print of the marriage contract are always unreadable. And always open to revision by forces stronger than a man's ego. The loveboat always leaks. And marriage is never a done deal.

I say he got off light. It could have been ponies or llamas or potbellied pigs. It would have been something. It always is.

ENVY IS PART OF THE SECRET LIFE.

In the *public* and *private* realms, envy has long been considered a sin infused with jealousy and a tendency to covet, which thou shalt not, especially in the case of thy neighbor's wife and whatever. Still, in the sanctuary of our solitude, we envy.

There are degrees of envy. The "Lord-I-wish-I-could-do-that" envy that is carried on with a light heart and good humor is harmless enough. Most envy that doesn't lead to theft and manslaughter is OK. Affirmative envy that reflects delight in the fringes of human achievement is a pleasure like bittersweet chocolate. You have to develop a taste for it.

In my case, I envy a guy who used to come into the old Buffalo Tavern in Seattle. He'd hang around the pool tables and offer to play you left-handed. Using a No. 5 trenching shovel for a cue. If you'd give him three balls ahead, he'd even play you with the digging end of the shovel, which had some duct tape on it to keep from nicking the cue ball. If you were smart and you weren't one hell of a pool player, you'd leave well enough alone. And just offer to watch him destroy some other fool's ego. But if you wanted to get a little education of the kind they don't teach in high school, and you didn't mind losing twenty dollars in a hurry, then you could take him on, shovel and all. I know about all this—firsthand.

Oh, he was good, all right, but he was nothing compared to his wife.

She played with a broom or a mop—your choice—no handicap.

She'd whipped every hotshot cue-pusher in town before she stopped playing pool and started having babies. Rumor is she played her obstetrician three rounds of eight ball for her bill, double or nothing. She won. My wife envied her.

My wife also envied Lena Horne, the tall, African-American, sexy, sultry torch singer who has graced the American stage for so long. My wife is short, Asian-American, sweet, and is good at old Girl Scout songs. It's OK that she envied Lena Horne. For this kind of envy, you don't go to hell.

* * *

At age fifty-five, I begin to realize there are some things I will never have or be or do. For lack of opportunity, equipment, inclination, talent, or something. Playing championship pool with a shovel or a broom or a mop is just not going to happen in my case. I'm stuck with the secret consolation of affirmative envy. My only hope is being reincarnated. I am counting big on reincarnation.

In my next life, I will be one of those who remembers great poetry and can recite it with skill and passion. I will be able to tie all kinds of knots and never forget how from one time to the next. When I come around again, I will have a brain that can become fluent in another language.

I will be able to play a small accordion, tap-dance, sing in a very deep bass voice, do close-up magic tricks, and play "As Time Goes By" on the slide trombone so well that all estranged lovers will be reunited when they hear it.

And I will finally be able to remember what beats what in a poker hand.

Note that I don't ask to be handsome or wise. Those are burdens I couldn't carry. Mostly, it's just the small stuff I envy now and want next time. Like being able to shoot championship pool with a shovel.

Or maybe with a chopstick.

Now *that* would be something.

*A*N ARTICLE IN *THE NEW YORK TIMES* GAVE THE price tag for a basic household tool kit. It suggested that the best buy was an all-in-one tool set, including a hammer, five pliers, nine screwdrivers, twelve combination wrenches, fourteen hex-key wrenches, an adjustable wrench, a forty-piece socket set, a seven-piece nut-driver set, a ten-foot measuring tape, a utility knife, a wire stripper, and a folding saw. In an aluminum case—$149.95 plus tax.

There was a time when I would have ordered two of these sets.

There was a time I thought tools made the man. There was a time when I thought if I couldn't actually own a hardware store, I'd at least like to live next door to one. That's the handyman's dream. On the other hand, if I had all the right tools and all the right parts, the obligation to always *use* the right tools and *employ* the correct parts might be inhibiting. It surely would take the creative edge off common home repair.

As a matter of fact, I already do have a great many of the right tools out in my garage somewhere, along with drawers full of proper parts. What I don't have is the time to make ten trips out to the garage or sort through the boxes and drawers. I begin to realize that these tools and parts are talismans—juju devices to appease the household gods. Besides, it's cold and dark out there in the garage.

But the real secret of efficient home repair is quite simple: Use what's handy when the need arises.

I give you an example. At least half your basic home fixit jobs call for a screwdriver. You don't really need to go out in the garage and spend ten minutes looking for that sixty-dollar twenty-piece matching set of screwdrivers with three styles of magnetic tips. Many screwdrivers are nearby. Fingernails. A dime, nickel, or quarter. But you really can't beat the all-purpose combination of a butter knife and a nail file. In fact, the kitchen is full of knives that make great screwdrivers. So what if you snap the tip off one? No problem—you've got yourself an improved screwdriver.

Spoons also work quite nicely when the knives don't. Even forks will pry the lids off cans, though forks should be reserved for mixing paint. The point is, you have at hand all the screwdrivers you'll ever need. Right there in the kitchen.

Need a lightweight saw? That's what serrated bread knives are for.

As to pliers; fingers. Or fingers with a dishtowel wrapped around the top of something that won't come off after you've pounded the edge of it with the handle end of a butcher knife. Tweezers and clothespins work as pliers for small jobs. But the best pliers are in your own mouth—teeth, of course, teeth. Just don't let your kids catch you.

And while I'm mentioning body parts, let's talk about *power* tools—knees, elbows, fists, and feet. A great many things can be fixed by kicking, pounding, shaking, and throwing.

To cut and open things, there are, of course, all those knives in the kitchen, and the razor blades and manicure sets in the bathroom, which is a good place to use them because you are closer to the Band-Aids, which you will need sooner or later when you use sharp tools.

* * *

Sandpaper? Emery boards for fine work, a cheese grater for the heavy projects. Nutmeg grater for finesse.

Duct tape. Duct tape is a must. No home, office, marriage, or life should be without it. You can never have too much duct tape. Did you know it's even required for all NASA missions in space? Seriously.

Just as basic are a pencil and a scratch pad—so you can leave a message for the repairman who comes when you have overrepaired something.

As for miscellaneous parts, don't go to a hardware store. Go to a garage sale when some retired couple is selling out and moving to Florida. Buy that drawerful of stuff they have in their kitchen somewhere. The one full of thirty years' worth of odds and ends. Most everything you'll ever need for home repair is in there.

See, the truth is, at home, in private and in secret, we mostly make do. That's how we run our lives most of the time. We might as well accept that. And feel good about it. And get good at it. It's a matter of attitude, as summarized in these nine rules from the Fulghum Guide to Being Handy Around the House:

1. Try to work alone. An audience is rarely any help.

2. Despite what you may have been told by your mother, praying and cursing are both helpful in home repair—but only if you are working alone.

3. Work in the kitchen whenever you can— many fine tools are there, it's warm and dry, and you are close to the refrigerator.

4. If it's electronic, get a new one, or consult a twelve-year-old.

5. Stay simpleminded. Plug it in, get a new battery, replace the bulb or the fuse, see if the tank is empty, try turning the "on" switch, or just paint over it.

6. Always take credit for miracles. If you dropped the alarm clock while taking it apart and it suddenly starts working, you have healed it.

7. If something looks level, it is level.

8. If at first you don't succeed, redefine success.

9. Above all, if what you've done is stupid, but it works, it ain't stupid.

*I*T'S AUGUST—A WEDNESDAY MORNING—AND I'M rolling down the road toward town and Moon's Barbershop. As I drive, I wonder if I'll ever be one of those old geezers who have nothing better to do than hang around the shop swapping tales. I hope so.

And when I glance up into the rearview mirror, I see I may be getting closer to geezerhood than I thought. I do have a few stories of my own. Maybe today I'll just take a chair after I get my haircut and lay out an adventure I had the summer I was seventeen. Maybe I should rehearse this—work on my geezer style and tone of voice.

"Let me tell you about moths. People around here say you better watch out for black-widow spiders, but I say moths is worse—they'll eat your clothes and cause fires. Them moths they're a lot more dangerous than you think. That's right, moths. You can get killed messing with moths. One damn near burned the bunkhouse down over at the Prade ranch one summer. I'll tell you. Me and two or three other boys were mending fence for Old Man Mickel that year.

"At night Rusty he liked to crank up the lamp and read to himself to get sleepy. But all the bugs in Carson County would come for the light and Rusty he spent most of his time swatting and whipping at bugs instead of reading. Just made him crazy. So one night, hot as it was, Rusty he closed every door and window in the bunkhouse and he stuffed newspapers and socks in every single hole and crack he could find where bugs could get in. Spent an hour doing it and worked up quite a sweat but said he didn't give a damn he'd sooner fry to death than go bug crazy.

"Anyhow, Rusty he put the lamp over by his bed and he got a *Life* magazine and rolled that sucker up for a club and he stood there by the bed and he beat hell out of the few stray bugs left in the room that was stupid enough to go for the lamp. It was a massacre. He beat the fur off them bugs, let me tell you. There was bug bodies in little pieces ever which way. He killed every last one of them. He thought.

"It got quiet and old Rusty he rolled himself a smoke and got himself an old *Reader's Digest* and settled down to bed to read in peace. He was just about asleep when this big gray fuzzy moth come from who-knows-where and went to circling the light and swooping down between Rusty and his *Reader's Digest* and Rusty he went to grabbing at it and slapping at it but he couldn't catch it or kill it. Well, I guess something just busted loose in his mind because the next thing I knew old Rusty he roared up out of the bed screaming and cussing and he run over into the next room and grabbed a piece of stovewood and come back hollering, 'I'LL TEACH YOU TO MESS WITH ME, YOU CORK-SCREWIN' SONOFABITCH!' And he run right across his bed and took a swat or two and missed, and the moth he flew up high and lit near to the ceiling higher than Rusty could reach so Rusty he went to beating on the wall and screaming, 'YOU'RE GONNA DIE, YOU'RE GONNA DIE,' at the moth.

"Rusty beat the wall until the moth flew off and went for the light again. Old Rusty he swung and missed the moth and hit the coal-oil lamp dead center like he was stroking for center field. Broke the lamp all to hell and splattered burning coal oil and splintered glass all over the east end of the bunkhouse. Rusty couldn't have done better with a stick of dynamite. Well, there was fire all over the wall and glass all over the floor and the rest of us come roaring up out of our beds, I'll tell you, and started running for buckets and a hose and shovels and hollering like dogs in a fight. We got the fire out, but not before it scorched up the bunkhouse pretty good. We was washing smoke out of our sheets and picking glass out of our feet for a week.

"Couple a days later Rusty was trying to read again and there's this big old gray moth come flittering onto his pillow. Rusty hollers, 'IT'S HIM, IT'S HIM, HE'S COME BACK FROM THE GRAVE!' But I don't know—even a moth ain't that stupid. Rusty hollers he's going to get his shotgun and blow this sucker clean to Jesus. I blew the lamp out about then. I didn't want to die before payday."

By the time I got to Moon's, I was fired up. I did it—got my haircut and then went out front where the geezers were sitting in old cane-bottom chairs on the sidewalk in the shade. I told my story. They laughed politely enough, in an indulgent sort of way. But it was the last story I got to tell. I had reminded them of even better tales, and they were off and running.

The truth was clear—I was an amateur among professionals. There's more to a performance than just the contents of the story. I'll have to learn how to hold my mouth just right, learn not to laugh at my own yarn, and develop a slumped, nonchalant lean while sitting in a chair. Guess I'll have to learn to spit, too. Real geezerhood may still be a way off for me.

OVER THE LAST COUPLE OF MONTHS, I HAVE RE-
ceived information from the following organizations:

The National Tattoo Association
The International Save the Pun Foundation
Clowns of America International
Burlington Liars' Club
Thimble Collectors International
National Association to Advance Fat Acceptance
Fairy Investigation Society
The Anti-Circumcision League
The International Federation of Tiddlywinks
    Associations
American Poultry Historical Society
Spark Plug Collectors of America

Count Dracula Fan Club
Bobs International
Snowdome Collectors' Association
Liberace Fan Club
National Pygmy Goat Association
The Howdy Doody Memorabilia Collectors
  Club
The American Fancy Rat and Mouse
  Association
The Flying Funeral Directors of America
Bat Conservation International
American Council of Spotted Asses, Inc.
American Roller Coaster Enthusiasts
Procrastinators' Club of America
The Society for the Investigation of the
  Unexplained

Membership in the last organization appealed to
me, because I had not solicited this remarkable pile
of mail and had a hard time explaining to my sec-
retary and wife how this barrage came about. I
could qualify for the Society for the Investigation
of the Unexplained.

At first, I found the brochures amusing, then amazing, then fascinating.

Most are serious organizations, and their existence could be taken seriously.

The right to freely associate and assemble is
what our country is about.

Here's proof at least that some of us are taking advantage of the privilege.

There must be thousands and thousands of organized groups—finding kinship around almost every human interest or point of view. These organizations illustrate our need for company—to know we are not entirely one of a kind, despite a paradoxical need to be unique.

I received material from one man who was the only member of his group. But he found there were others who also belonged to one-person groups, so he now heads up the International Association of Single-Minded Rogue Males and One Person Clubs.

As the unsolicited mail continued to pour in, I realized this had to be the work of a practical joker. One of my friends had set me up. I had three in mind. The three friends with the most complex senses of mischief, who always operate on the other side of the conventional. Not wanting to tip my hand, I carefully stalked the suspects for weeks.

When I was sure I knew which of my friends submitted my name to all these groups, I sent in *his* name and the membership fees and joined him up to all of them.

The tables are turned on him.

But no. The *joke* is on *me*.

I guessed the wrong friend.

And the guy I did join to all these groups is as blown away by his membership mail as I was. Congratulations to him! There are now *two* members of the Where-the-Hell-Did-This-Come-From? Mystery Mail Association. Welcome to our club!

*F*OR MOST OF MY LIFE, I HAVE KNOWN VERY FEW people with my last name, Fulghum (full-jum). My immediate family was small and died off early, leaving me the last apple on this branch of the family tree. As a result of recent genealogical research on the part of several distant relatives, it became clear that anybody with our last name was kinfolk. For the last several years we have held a national reunion. There are enough Robert Fulghums to form a baseball team.

As you might expect, as we have assembled our family tree, much attention is paid to the more famous figures of the past to whom we are supposedly related. Viking sea-rovers, kings, crusaders, knights, dukes, and those who accompanied conquerors and invaders hither and yon.

But I'm not really so sure we should be so proud of all of these guys. Weren't they greedy pillagers and plunderers who made war on innocent people? Weren't they feudal landlords who oppressed the peasants? Weren't they migrant exploiters looking for something for nothing?

And how about the women—it bothers me that the great women are left out of the family hall of heroes.

In addition to the exemplars, I'd also bet our family has had its share of chowderheads, liars, chicken thieves, pickpockets, cowards, bad cooks, and fools.

The truth is, the great majority of those whose genes we bear were pretty ordinary folks. They stayed at home and minded their own business, thus we don't know their names or much about their lives. They were more like us present-day Fulghums than the headliners across the centuries.

I wonder what it was like, back there in the good old days.

I imagine me in April 992, a thousand years ago.

The tenth century. A century in the middle of what modern historians call the Dark Ages. A century whose only illumination was sun, moon, lightning, fire, and starlight. Whose only source of power was human or animal muscle and falling water. My name would be something like Robert the Crazy-Legged (Norman French: *fol-jambe*).

Likely I would have spent the night sleeping on the floor on filthy straw, wrapped in lice-ridden cloaks, in the same room with my wife, nine children, three brothers, one sister, my mother-in-law, my great-aunt, and several orphaned children.

I live in a connected series of mud-and-wattle huts, also shared at night with two cows, two pigs, some ducks, chickens, and several dogs

I have been awakened by a chicken pecking vermin off the rags wrapped around my head.

After breakfast of hard, stale, dirt-colored bread and a gray gruel, I will go out in the same clothes I slept in to the fields of the lord of the domain and push a board plow all day in the rain; records show it rained a great deal in the tenth century. It will take two of my sons and my wife to pull the plow through the sodden fields. My thoughts are not particularly noble.

"When do I eat?"

"I think I will kick the chickens."

"It is raining again."

"I am sick and tired."

"Let's eat a chicken."

Every day I worry that at any moment I will be swept up in some small war that is always going on in the neighborhood, or that armed brigands will carry away my livestock or my wife and children.

Every day I worry that the lord of the domain will call me up to fight and die somewhere, or else will send his men to collect even more of his share of my crops than had been agreed.

I work until dark, six days a week, fifty-two weeks of the year, with no vacation or sick leave.

At night, I and my kinfolk huddle around the smoldering fire of wet wood, scratch flea bites, pick lice, eat gruel, and wonder why everybody in the huts across the river died last week.

I will lie down again in my clothes in exhausted sleep, hungry, as I have for as long as I can remember. Not starving, just hungry.

No doctor or dentist is available to me. I can't read or write or do arithmetic. Sex and elimination are urges that are satisfied where and when they occur.

On Sunday, because it is required, I trudge off to the small chapel several miles away to hear a sermon of hellfire and damnation. I can believe in the wrath of an angry God—my daily life is a continual reminder that I must have fallen from grace. Famine, flood, drought, plague, pestilence, taxes, war, filth, and an early death are as constant as the coming of another day.

After holy services, I might find a friend who has a hogshead of sour beer, get drunk, and brawl with sticks until I get knocked into a ditch, am fined, and am dragged home by the bailiff, to awake to another day with a chicken pecking at my head.

This life is a narrow, brutish struggle for daily

existence, with all my human energies exhausted in the mere attempt to stay alive. Yet I actually have a better life than many.

Things are fairly simple and uncomplicated, if that's any use.

I do not have to worry about the meaning of life or the events of the world beyond what I can see from my front door. The church has explanations for every question that might arise in my simple mind. And I believe it's true that someday I will go to heaven, where everything will be quite wonderful. There are no chickens in heaven, or so I am told and so I am glad to believe.

And I will not have long to wait until heaven. Forty years is a very long life in the tenth century. Most likely I will be gone before that—from starvation, infection, plague, war, or just the wear and tear of it all.

My gene strain survived those hard times.

The famous relatives back there don't impress me nearly as much as those nameless, hang-tough members of the family who survived on sheer grit. I'm proud to be their heirs.

I think of them when I get knocked down by circumstances in my own life.

And I get up and go on again, in the memory of tough company, for the sake of those who come after me.

*I*NNER CONVERSATIONS WITH MYSELF—BETWEEN ME and my dummy—and me and my committee—are often confusing to me. They would be even more so to an observer. But these are the conversations that take place in that secret room where the hard work is done. I want to speak from there. Perhaps putting the conversations into a self-interview form will help:

"What's the best meal you've ever eaten?"

"Chicken broth and saltine crackers."

"Come on, get serious."

"I kid you not. At a New Year's party about ten years ago, I drank most of a bottle of Greek brandy—at the same time that I was unknowingly incubating the worst case of influenza I've ever had. By morning I had an O-God-help-me-help-me-and-I-won't-ever-do-it-again hangover simultaneously with the Hong Kong flu. My head hurt so bad I moaned every time I moved. I spent hours in the shower throwing up and throwing down. My body ached so bad I cried. For four days, I thought I was going to die. I welcomed death.

"Late on the fifth night, I began to feel hungry. At three o'clock in the morning, I cautiously risked a teaspoonful of hot chicken broth and one saltine cracker. Yes ... OK! Suddenly, I knew my ordeal was over. Anything going down was not coming back up.

"So I had a whole potful of chicken broth and a whole box of crackers. Nothing, nothing, ever tasted as good to me. Best meal I ever ate."

"The best feelings in your life come when you start feeling good after you've been feeling just awful."

"True for all crises—small and large."

"Tell about a large one."

"How about the time I tried committing suicide? Twenty-five years ago.

"A harsh time. Everything on my plate seemed foul and rancid—job, marriage, career, friendships, family life, and future.

"Ironic that I was a volunteer at the time on a twenty-four-hour answering service for a crisis center. Desperate people called in the middle of the night and said they were considering suicide. I resigned my post when I began to think they were on the right track. Getting dead began to seem like a good idea to me."

"What did you do?"

"One morning—one Monday morning—I just ran away from home. Got in my car, drove to the airport, and caught the next plane leaving. It was going to Texas, the last place I had in mind, but since Texas was where I grew up, probably the place I unconsciously wanted to be—back to the beginning—to complete the circle or find where things started going wrong—or something—I don't know . . ."

"What did you do when you got there?"

"Tried to buy a gun, but there was a waiting period if you were from out of state. So shooting myself was out. Which was OK with me because I didn't really want to shoot myself and make a mess somebody else had to deal with."

"What next?"

"I looked for something to jump off of, but there wasn't anyplace high enough in that part of Texas, and then there was the mess factor again.

"Two days had gone by. While I was working out the technical problems of getting dead, I was driving around in a rented car looking at the scenery of my childhood. If I told you what I was thinking, I'd be making it up. Because I don't remember. It was a dream in a way and a serious review of my past in another, but words don't apply—I was way down in the basement of my soul somewhere.

"My plan jelled. I bought a vacuum-cleaner hose and some wide masking tape. That night I drove out in the plains for a couple of hundred miles, turned off on a dirt road, and drove farther. I parked. Tried taping the hose to the exhaust pipe and then in through a wing window of the car."

"What was going on in your mind then?"

"It felt like a contest between three people.

"One wanted to get it over with. Another seemed to think it was funny, and the third was obsessed with the taping problems, never mind the consequences. I remember the conversation, along the lines of—'Can't you hurry up,' 'He'll never do it,' and 'The only problem is this tape you bought.'

"The trouble was that the hose was round and the exhaust pipe was oval, and I had to make the connection by using lots of tape to span the difference in shape. When I ran the engine, the heat of the exhaust melted the adhesive on the tape, and the hose fell off.

"It was funny. How absurd. Too dumb to do something so simple right. I was protected from myself by my own incompetence. I began to laugh. I couldn't even kill myself. I laughed to the point of hysteria, which turned into sobbing grief, which turned into silence broken by renewed laughter. Maybe I could just sit here and die of stupidity. I could see the headlines. MAN MANAGES TO DUMB HIMSELF TO DEATH——SUCCUMBS TO EXHAUSTION BROUGHT ON BY TOO MANY FAILED ATTEMPTS TO DO AWAY WITH HIMSELF.

"Man too dumb to live——that's me.

"But what if I had succeeded? I had this vision of my corpse sitting up at the wheel of this rented car out here in the bushes in the middle of nowhere——and the world going on without me—— and it seemed like such a meaningless thing to do.

"And I began to think of my ancestors—— considering that I was alive now because a lot of men and women before me had been able to take whatever life threw at them and go on. My genes had been through the Dark Ages, through the Black Death, across oceans to an unknown land, through wars and bad marriages and bankruptcy and all kinds of defeats that made my problems seem like a picnic. Toughness was permanently engraved on my genes. How could I give up here? How could I throw all that away?

"I began to laugh again. Death isn't what I wanted. It wasn't *less* life I wanted, but *more* life——life with meaning. And if I wanted something to laugh about, I had found that, all right: me, forever me——no bigger fool than I.

"And I never felt better in my life than at that moment. The best feeling in the world comes when you start feeling good again after you've been feeling awful."

* * *

"So then what happened?"

"Returning home after running away to kill myself was really awkward. For one thing, I was in a great, exuberant, life-affirming mood. I felt like Lazarus after his resurrection.

"On the other hand, I had upset my family and friends, and I expected a stormy scene with my wife. Oddly enough, she was calm. On reflection, I suspect she probably had wished at times that I would just disappear or drop dead. When it seemed like that's exactly what I'd done, she went through a reality check of her own.

"Her response was a complete surprise.

"She had bought me a glad-you-came-back-alive gift.

"A canary. A yellow, living, singing canary.

"I'm not a pet person. Yet here was this beautiful bird hanging in a brass wire cage in the window of my room—singing as though the joy itself were distilled in its song. How absurd! How wonderfully right. I remember shouting at it, 'SING, BIRD, SING!'

"Within a year the marriage ended, and the bird escaped while its cage was being cleaned. But I'll always love the mother of my children for the gift of empathetic grace in the form of that canary, which still sings in the sunniest window of my soul and welcomes me home from my ongoing bullfights."

"Bullfights? What bullfights? Tell me about the bullfights."

"When I was a young man, I accompanied my father on a business trip to Mexico. We went to the Plaza de Toros in Mexico City to see the bullfights. A wonderfully terrifying experience. And embarrassing. Experiencing in public the fear and blood and death and the mad energy of the crowd was too close to images of terror and loathing I had concealed in my nightmares and fantasy. I cried.

"This powerful experience has kept me attached to bullfighting over the years, though I have never again been to a live event. I've read many books, collected photographic essays, seen movies, and talked with afficionados and two professional matadors.

"It is not that I like bullfighting as such. But it's the clearest metaphor I have in my mind for dealing with the dark, dangerous demon of death that runs loose in the arena of my mind from time to time.

"With experience and practice, one may increase the odds in favor of triumphing over the bull. I respect the bull. I know that even the best matadors come close to death. And sometimes—sometimes—the bull wins.

"My bull is the beast of self-destruction. I know he's in there, always.

"But at age fifty-five, I am at the top of my form as a matador.

"I'm confident in the presence of the bull.

"This confidence is called *ver llegar* in the ring. It means 'to watch them come.' It is the ability to plant your feet exactly so—to hold your ground and see calmly, as in slow motion, the charge of the bull, knowing that you have what it takes to maneuver the bull safely by. This is dynamic stability. Standing still is one of the steps in dancing, as moments of silence are part of music. Confidence lies in the stillness. It is the confidence that comes from many passes and many fights—you can control the bull and defeat it because you have done it before.

"My bull comes at me when I have succumbed to examining my life with a microscope. Little mites become dragons under the lens, and fear makes me weak. Or the bull comes when I am hurriedly trying to collect and carry all the baggage of my life and haul it up the spiral staircase that leads to nowhere, and I despair of the absurdity of my life. The bull comes then. Because he thinks I welcome him as a kind of solution.

"I know him now. I can smell him, sense him before he moves. I welcome him. Yah, Toro, come on. I plant my feet and watch him come. He charges. I pass him safely by with a swing of the cape of my confidence. The crowd in my head roars. OLÉ! The crowd is made up of all those ancestors who passed their bulls—they are pulling for me. OLÉ! OLÉ! OLÉ!

"There is always a silence when the bull is defeated."

"And in that silence, the bird in the window sings again?"

"Yes."

IN 1984 MY WIFE AND I SHOULDERED OUR BACK-packs and set off on a five-month journey around the world. A dream come true. A wonder wander walkabout. The romantic anticipation came easy—the reality was often hard.

Traveling is anxious work. So much time is absorbed in just coping with the unfamiliar—with language, currency, local customs and officials, accommodations, and food. The trouble with "Getting Away from It All" is that you indeed get away from it all—all those background comforts of home—as well as from the unconscious ease with familiar smells, sounds, and cultural patterns. Having all your mental systems on full alert for a long time is exhausting. One gets cranky. And two get even crankier.

Our adventure fatigue was relieved by an elephant ride in Thailand.

This came at the midpoint of our journey, when we were thinking, If we're having such a wonderful time, why aren't we having a wonderful time?

An acquaintance arranged for us to visit a forest reserve north of Chiang Mai where elephants are still used for all the heavy work of logging. We were to view the operation from elephant back. A shaky ladder was tilted against the side of an elephant. We cautiously climbed up and onto an equally shaky wooden platform strapped to the elephant's back. The anxiety of getting on was matched by the anxiety of riding. We were a long way off the ground, and it felt as if we would be catapulted in that direction at any moment by the great lurching march of the beast.

When the ladder was raised again for us to get off, I noticed a small sign attached to the top step.

NOTICE: INSTRUCTIONS FOR DISMOUNTING FROM
ELEPHANT.
FIRST, COMPOSE YOUR MIND.
MUCH EASIER TO GET DOWN THAN UP.

In the ensuing years, much of that trip around the world has faded from conscious memory. But indelibly written in the operating instructions for my life is that admonition from the top rung of that ladder in Thailand. The instructions continued, concerning holding on with both hands and not poking the elephant. But it was that first line that spoke to me.

Even now, when I am about to make a move of consequence, small or large, a warning light flashes from the control panel in my head: "This is an elephant dismount." And sometimes, sometimes, I actually manage to compose my mind.

SOCCER MANIA COMES TO OUR SEATTLE NEIGHBOR-
hood every September.

When children appear at the door selling luxury
candy bars to make money to buy their own uniforms, we know the soccer season is under way.
These ill-at-ease visitors on the front porch are the
rookies, both at the game of soccer and the game
of door-to-door sales.

Here's the tableau:

A timid knock at the door. A small child. Head
down, muttering, hand holding out the bar of chocolate as if apologetically returning something stolen.

The child does not want to be there.

The parent, standing off in the bushes, does not
want to be there.

And you do not need the chocolate.

But since you were once the child and several times the parent in this semi-scam, you are obliged to take your place in this initiation of the young into entrepreneurial capitalism, sports, and the American Way.

(Besides, while it is true that you don't really *need* the chocolate, you *want* the chocolate, and it feels so right to simultaneously help the young and get candy.)

The nine-year-old daughter of a friend recently went through this coming-of-age ritual in a way that was both disastrous and triumphant.

Since this was the first season for her team, each child was obliged to help raise money for uniforms by taking at least one case of chocolate bars to sell. A model of soccer-team spirit—everybody plays a part in achieving a goal.

With no enthusiasm whatever, the girl accepted her case of chocolate in the same spirit she would accept pimples in a few years—something to be avoided if possible, but endured if necessary. She wanted to play ball. She didn't know retail sales was a prerequisite, but so be it.

Her mother and father did not buy the whole case outright from her as she had hoped. So much for Plan A.

Her brother and his friends were no help, though they tried to help her diminish her inventory by stealing a couple of bars. And every member of her Sunday School class also had chocolate to sell.

She hid the chocolate under her bed for a week, hoping a fairy would take it and leave the money. No luck.

When the soccer-league candy chairmother called the father to find out what was going on and why the child had neither come to soccer practice nor produced the chocolate receipts, the father's pride was hooked. He promised results.

He gave his daughter an emergency-level intensive course in salesmanship and personal responsibility. He and the daughter rehearsed. She came to the door and practiced knocking and he shouted, "KNOCK LOUDER, I CAN'T HEAR YOU!" until she could hit the door like the first wave of a police raid.

He made her look up, speak plainly, and offer a two-for-one deal if necessary. When he finally got her to shout, *"BUY THIS CANDY OR I WILL SET YOUR HOUSE ON FIRE!"* he figured assertiveness training had gone far enough. He marched her off with fire in her belly. She was pumped!

At the first house, her father gave her a go-get-'em pat on the butt and hid behind a tree to watch the kid pitch candy. The child stood at the door without moving for five agonizing minutes until her father realized the fire in her belly had burned out. He rescued her, and they walked back home in silence.

The father gave her a new pep talk about doing hard things and having courage and how it was when he was a little boy. He appealed to her place in the future of feminism. Real women can do this, OK? OK. All right, let's get 'em!

This time she wanted to go alone—her father lurking around on the sidelines made her nervous.

At the first house, she did her door-pounding and then ran for it.

Several other neighbors wondered who pounded at their door and disappeared. Unable to go beating on doors, the child spent the rest of the afternoon in the garage, hunkered down in the backseat of the family sedan. She reappeared at dinnertime, defeated.

The father couldn't give up. Too much was on the line. Crucial time in the life of his child. He considered the power of advertising. Take advantage of location. The family lived in a university town, in a neighborhood where football fans parked their cars on the way to the stadium for the Saturday afternoon games. Hundreds of people walked by. They would want and need candy!

The father explained the concept of advertising to his daughter and convinced her that all they had to do was make a sign, and she could stand down there on the street corner for an hour before the football game and the fans would buy all the candy she had.

They made a sign. HELP THE HILLSIDE SOCCER TEAM BUY UNIFORMS—$1.00—GREAT CHOCOLATE!

The little girl was gone for an hour. Her father could see her from the front porch and checked on her from time to time. She was selling candy hand over fist. Yes! YES!!

She came home smiling. A triumphant smile. She had sold *ALL* the chocolate—the whole case. She was relieved. Her father was proud of her and pleased with himself. What a team they made! They celebrated with a banana split, with extra chocolate sauce.

A couple of days later, their next-door neighbor, who had been a party to this adventure in retail sales, came over in the evening at that hour when children are already in bed. He and the father sat out on the front porch and had a beer while they enjoyed the autumn sky. The neighbor said, "I have something to show you. It's too good to keep, but you have to promise not to show it to your daughter."

From out of a brown paper grocery bag, the neighbor took a folded piece of cardboard. "I found this in my garbage can."

It was the sign the father had made for the daughter. It still said HELP THE HILLSIDE SCHOOL SOCCER TEAM BUY UNIFORMS—$1.00—GREAT CHOCOLATE. But underneath those words, in his daughter's crayoned printing, was this footnote:

"MY FATHER MADE ME DO THIS."

WHEN I TAUGHT PHILOSOPHY, I BEGAN THE COURSE by walking into the room after the students were seated and announcing, "We are now going to play musical chairs." The only further instruction was, "Please arrange your chairs and get ready to play."

No student ever asked why. Ever. And no student ever asked how to play.

They knew the rules as surely as they knew hide-and-seek.

Always the same response—the students enthusiastically arranged the chairs in a line with the seats alternating directions, then stood encircling the row of chairs. Ready, ready, ready!

All I had to do was punch up "Stars and Stripes Forever" on the tape machine, and the students marched around the chairs. Mind you, these were seniors in high school. They hadn't played musical chairs since second grade. But they still knew how, and jumped into the game without hesitation. Musical chairs! All right!

After removing a few chairs, I stopped the music. There was a mad scramble for the remaining chairs. Those without chairs were stunned. They knew how this game worked—music stops, get a chair—how could they not have a chair so soon? They had "How dumb can I be?" written on their faces.

Too bad. But they were losers. Out. Over against the wall. Only a game.

Music continues, students march around, chairs removed, STOP!

Students go crazy trying to get a chair this time.

As the game goes on, the quest for chairs turns serious. Then rough.

Girls are not going to fight jocks for chairs. Losers to the wall.

Down to two members of the wrestling team, who are willing to push, knee, kick, or bite to be the last person in a chair. This is war! STOP! And by jerking the chair out from under his opponent, one guy slams down into the last chair—a look of triumph on his face—hands raised high with forefingers signaling NUMBER ONE, NUMBER ONE.

The last student in the last chair always acted as if the class admired him and his accomplishment. He got the CHAIR! "I'm a WINNER!" Wrong.

Those losers lined up against the wall thought he was a jerk.

Admiration? Hardly. Contempt is what they felt.

This was not a game. Games were supposed to be fun.

This got too serious too fast—like high school life—and real life.

Did they want to play again? A few of the jocks did. But not the rest of the class. It all came back to them now. Big deal.

I insisted. Play one more time. With one rule change. Musical chairs as before, but this time, if you don't have a chair, sit down in someone's lap. Everybody stays in the game—it's only a matter of where you sit.

The students are thinking—well . . . OK.

Chairs are reset. Students stand ready. Music starts and they march. Chairs are removed. STOP! There is a pause in the action. The students are really thinking it over now. *(Do I want a chair to myself? Do I want to sit on someone's lap or have someone sit in mine? And who?)* The class gets seated, but the mood has changed. There is laughter— giggling. When the game begins again, there is a change of pace. Who's in a hurry?

When the number of chairs is sufficiently reduced to force two to a chair, a dimension of grace enters in as the role of sittee or sitter is clarified—"Oh, no, please, after you." Some advance planning is evident as the opportunity to sit in the lap of a particular person is anticipated.

As the game continues, and more and more people must share one chair, a kind of gymnastic dance form develops. It becomes a group accomplishment to get everybody branched out onto knees. Students with organizational skills come to the fore—it's a people puzzle to solve now—"Big people on the bottom first—put your arms around him—sit back—easy, easy."

When there is one chair left, the class laughs and shouts in delight as they all manage to use one chair for support now that they know the weight can be evenly distributed. Almost always, if they tumbled over, they'd get up and try again until everyone was sitting down. A triumphant moment for all, teacher included.

The only person who had a hard time with this paradigm shift was the guy who won the first time under the old rules. He lost his bearings—didn't know what winning was now.

As a final step to this process, I would tell the class we would push on one more round. "The music will play, you will march, and I will take away the last chair. When the music stops, you will all sit down in a lap."

"Can't be done," they say.

"Yes, it can," say I.

So once more they marched and stopped—what now?

"Everyone stand in a perfect circle.

"All turn sideways in place, as if you were going to walk together in a circle.

"Take a single step into the middle so as to have a tight circle now, with each person in the group bellyside to backside with the person ahead of them.

"Place your hands on the hips of the person in front of you.

"On the count of three, very carefully guide the person onto your knees at the same time as you very carefully sit down on the knees of the person behind you.

"Ready. One. Two. Three. Sit."

They all sat. No chair.

I have played the chair game in this way with many different groups of many ages in varied settings. The experience is always the same. It's a problem of sharing diminishing resources. This really isn't kid stuff. And the questions raised by musical chairs are always the same:

Is it always to be a winners-losers world, or can we keep everyone in the game?

Do we still have what it takes to find a better way?

SOME TANGIBLE EVIDENCE OF THE SECRET LIFE IS OF-
ten close at hand, or, in the case of men's wallets,
close behind. If a man wearing jeans walks toward
you on the street, step aside and take a look at his
stern as he passes you. You will notice this fat,
squarish lump riding at an angle in a hip pocket.
There is a permanent wearmark showing the position of the wallet, whether the man and wallet are
in the jeans at the moment or not. Even underneath
a suit coat, the leather lump and the wearmark are
inevitably there.

Unlike women, who tend to change purses to
match shoes or occasion, men usually have one
wallet, worn under all circumstances, whether it be
to clean out a septic tank or attend a wedding.
Consequently, the effects of sweat, body heat, and

time give the wallet a warped, lumpish shape more like a detachable leather wart than a billfold. It fits one place on one butt for all seasons and occasions. I tried putting a friend's wallet in my hip pocket and had this vague sense that all was not well with my world.

The importance of a wallet is emphasized by how a man feels when he has lost his wallet. It's a major emergency far beyond the value of any one item and far beyond the fact that most of the so-called valuable stuff, which can be replaced, is not really the most valuable stuff at all. Considered in this light, wallets may serve as the common key to the bank vaults of the secret lives of men.

I was asked to conduct a seminar for the senior members of a department of the federal government in Washington, D.C. Held in the solemn marble atmosphere of one of those classic Greco-Roman office buildings. The participants came wearing facades as serious as the building.

Middle-aged men, in dark suits, white shirts, quietly patriotic ties, dark socks, and polished shoes. Whatever hair they had was short and trim. Respectable in every way, they came bearing serious leather briefcases. Their demeanor was impressive if not downright intimidating. These men were running the United States government. They had no time to waste on frivolous entertainment. The message to me was clear: This seminar had better be worthwhile.

"A simple request, gentlemen: Please take out your wallets and place them on the table in front of you."

And out of that niche on their sterns came the fat old leather hamburgers—molded and moldy from years of use. They laughed. Their covers were blown.

"Now, please, take everything out of your wallet and spread it out on the table in front of you."

I was surprised at how willingly they complied. Their interest was piqued—*they* didn't *know* what was in there any more than I did.

The usual utilitarian items appeared: cash, credit cards, driver's licenses, and membership cards. In many cases, several of these items had expired and were no longer valid.

The bulk of the remaining material had the makings of a scrapbook. Business cards that came from meetings of months and years ago. Odds and ends of paper on which were written lists of things to get or do or buy, names of mechanics and repair services. And mystery information—again and again the murmur would come—"I've no idea where this came from or what it means or why it's in here."

Most had some little tiny scraps of paper on which were written those numbers you are not supposed to carry in a wallet: pin numbers for bankcard machines, long-distance credit card codes, the combination to a safe, private phone numbers, computer-access codes, locker numbers, and Social Security numbers. All written as tiny as possible on tiny pieces of paper, as if microscopic detail would confuse the finder of a lost or stolen wallet. Most men had to get out their reading glasses to read their own hieroglyphics; their eyes, like their memories, needed help. And again came the murmur—"I don't know what this is for."

And sure enough, a certain cultural myth proved to be based on fact—several men did indeed have a condom in their wallets. Still wrapped in the original packaging, but like much else in the wallets, showing signs of having been there a long time—like since junior high school—and provoking about the same level of raucous locker-room joking as they had in junior high.

Almost all of the men carried photographs. Worn, faded photographs. Nothing recent. Just the pictures of their children and wives when they were young. Little boys and little girls, posed and smiling in vulnerable innocence. Wives in hairdos of another time. Family groups: a mother and father once young, now old or dead and gone. Dogs. Cats. And a goat—supposedly a picture of a family pet, though the other men claimed it was his most recent girlfriend.

These photographs changed the atmosphere in the room. The men shared them, told the where-are-they-now stories—some of joy and accomplishment, some of sorrow and failure. The only recent photographs were of grandchildren, which of course led to the swapping of tales of precocious promise and pride.

In the meantime, the men had, of their own volition, loosened their ties and taken off their suit jackets as they opened up their private lives without me.

Not everyone was willing to share everything. I noticed some items being discreetly withheld—the photograph of a current lover—a state secret? Who knows? Even the bank of the secret life has safe-deposit boxes.

One man—the oldest and most respectably dressed of the lot—a man who, I learned later, was within a week of retirement, had not opened his wallet or relaxed enough to remove his jacket. He had not eliminated himself from the group discussion, but he was not sharing. His colleagues teased him into emptying his wallet.

For openers, he took out three brand-new condoms. There was a razzing cheer from the group. They gave him a standing ovation.

He held up his hand for attention and said,

"You're never too old, boys—never give up hope."
And the ovation continued.

As our seminar rambled on toward its close, I was
amazed and amused to notice that every one of
them—no exceptions—carefully put everything
back into his wallet—every last scrap. And, out of
long-practiced habit, each man leaned slightly forward and to one side and replaced this old talis-
manic scrapbook back where it belonged. These
were not just wallets after all. A wallet is a life
preserver—found, as usual, under the seat.

WHEN I THINK OF STAFF MEETINGS, BOARD MEETings, or time served on almost any committee, I think of the one man who triumphed over "meeting madness." The man whose style I sometimes wish I had.

David Dugan was his name. Though he had a college degree in civil engineering, and though he read history for pleasure, he enjoyed the pose of the simpleminded common man. Popeye was his model.

While in college, he had started as right defensive tackle on the football team for four years. After college he made his living as a heavy construction contractor, specializing in sewer systems and pipelines. He ran his life and business the way he played football—straight ahead up the middle, full power, nothing fancy.

Plainspoken in his conversation, he used one adjective: "sumbitch." After you got used to it, you didn't notice when he spoke of his "sumbitch" wife and his "sumbitch" kids and his "sumbitch" friends any more than when he spoke of the "sumbitch" government and the "sumbitch" Russians. He varied the tone a little, but it was all "sumbitch" to him.

I met him at a poker game. I liked him right away. He came to church the next Sunday saying he'd never heard a sumbitch poker player preach. He stayed on to become an active member of the church. We found him kind and generous behind his facade. His laughter kept us loose in tense moments, and his resources kept us in business when we needed help. Dugan's way was large, and he didn't hold back when it came to his part in the life of the church. If we had some trash to haul, he'd drive up in a four-ton dump truck. He sent a road grader to move some gravel around, and to fetch a Christmas tree he sent a diesel truck hitched to a Low Boy trailer—the kind used to transport bulldozers. For Dugan there were very few of life's problems that could not be addressed with heavy equipment and a go-get-'em attitude.

Dugan lured me to his construction site one fall with the promise of being allowed to drive a D8 Caterpillar tractor. Sitting in his office trailer drinking coffee, he astonished me by throwing open his briefcase to reveal bundles and bundles of hundred-dollar bills, and a .38-caliber pistol. It was like being in a movie when the bank robbers were about to split the loot. Not to worry. He explained that because his projects were often far from town and he had to hire a lot of temporary labor, he made his payroll in cash. He was bonded to carry as much as half a million dollars. And licensed to carry the gun to protect himself.

Because he was often away for long stretches of time, Dugan refused an invitation to serve as an officer of the board of trustees. But when he was in town, he came to board meetings anyhow. He thought he ought to contribute to the life of the church beyond just sitting in a pew, and he wanted to know what was going on from the source, not the newsletter.

As is often the case, "Member of the Board of Trustees" sounds like an important honor, when in fact, the work of a board is more often mundane than not. During the year when Dugan attended meetings, the board's entire time and energy was devoted to a leaking roof, parking problems, and the difficulty of getting wholesale prices for paper towels and toilet paper. Dugan never said a word. He listened—with chagrin written on his face.

One January evening the board shifted to an

even more fascinating problem. On the *entrance* side of the church, the driveway had developed potholes. Patching had not helped, so it seemed the driveway would have to be repaved. An expensive proposition. However, on the *exit* side, nearest the church school, the driveway was smooth, encouraging a level of speed thought dangerous to children. Speed bumps would have to be built there and signs posted. More expense.

Three hours had drained away while every possible dimension of this driveway problem had been considered. No solution in sight, the meeting fumbled on.

From his seat outside the board circle, Dugan raised his hand to make a proposal. "Leave the potholes on the entrance side and dig potholes on the exit side. Spray a little tar in them. Call them "speedholes." He could do it with a shovel and a couple of cans of hot tar in a couple of hours. Free.

The board gnawed on the problem for another hour—worried about being sued and what the neighbors would think.

In exasperation Dugan stood up, placed his briefcase on the table, and asked forcefully, "What's this sumbitch church worth—the whole sumbitch thing, buildings, land, everything—gimme a round figure."

They didn't know about the briefcase.

The church treasurer replied, "Oh, maybe three hundred thousand dollars."

"Great," said Dugan, "I'm gonna buy the sumbitch!"

And he opened his briefcase, laid his pistol aside, and began throwing out bundles of hundred-dollar bills until he reached the established price.

Silence—stunned silence.

"Gimme the deed, and it's done," said Dugan.

"What are you going to do with it?" someone asked.

"I'm going to get my crew and equipment over here, and we'll level the sumbitch and haul it to the sumbitch dump before sundown. And I'll use the land for the cemetery you guys are headed toward in these meetings of the living dead. I'm going to put up a sumbitch monument to the Unknown God."

"What's the gun for, Dugan?" an anxious member asked.

"I was thinking about putting every last one of you sumbitches out of your misery. Too bad it's against the law."

Then he chewed the board members up one side and down the other for not spending their time on important things and how he came to church for religion and what he got was pissant construction workers he wouldn't hire for a day, and bygod if they decided they wanted to get serious about all the things a church ought to be doing in this world, to bygod sumbitch let him know.

Packing up his money and his gun, he stomped

off out the door, shouting from down the hall, "The sumbitch offer still stands."

What Dugan said and did had a familiar ring to it.

For all those who have the noble work of the world to do, the question is essentially the same, yes? Fish or cut bait? Dream or do?

Dugan's acts are nothing new in religious circles. The prophet Jeremiah didn't use quite those same words, but his sumbitch message was about the same. Woe unto you, you sumbitches! Shape up or die! Get serious or get out of the way!

No, we didn't dig the speedholes. Just too simple a solution.

But there were more than a few times that the board members thought they'd made a great mistake—they should have sold the sumbitch.

WHEN I SPEAK BEFORE EDUCATIONAL GROUPS, I tell my "war stories"—those tales that come out of my life as a schoolteacher. When teachers ask me how I feel about my current vocation, I reply that sometimes I feel sorry for myself—when I've been traveling too long and spent too much time in the public fishbowl, and I'm tired and lonely and depressed. The self-pity doesn't last long—because a little voice in the back of my head always reminds me, "You *could* be at a faculty meeting."

Faculty meetings are black holes that suck intelligence out of nice people's minds. I hated them so much I always sat on the floor in the back of the room and concentrated on sleeping with my eyes open. Sometimes I survived by imagining what everybody in the room looked like sitting there in their underwear.

Once I almost died in a faculty meeting. I had taken a paring knife to school to sharpen in the school shop and had put the paring knife in the outside pocket of my book satchel, which was next to me on the floor when I fell over laughing at some absurd thing. I drove the knife through the fleshy part of the back side of my right arm and into my rib cage. It wasn't as serious a wound as it seems, but I passed out from shock and lay there on the floor. Nobody paid me any attention until blood started seeping out onto the rug.

An ambulance was called, and I was hauled away to be stitched up.

The event entered into the mythology of faculty life. "Fulghum hated faculty meetings so much he tried to kill himself during one."

It took a while for the chairman of the meeting, the young assistant headmaster, to believe I wasn't faking when I did my hara-kiri act and fell over. He believed I would do anything to get out of a faculty meeting, and here was proof. His suspicion was well founded. It was true.

He'd also remembered his previous experience with me and the ape and the naked lady. And that's a long story and a half—one that begins way out in left field and wanders all over the landscape. I like telling it because it's such a different story when seen from the viewpoint of each one of the participants. It has philosophical dimensions, as well. The story begins at a wedding.

A grand garden wedding in early summer. If a wedding inspector had stopped by, she would have found nothing amiss. Though she might have wondered why the bride and the groom and the minister grinned on the edge of laughter all through the ceremony. It was because the groom had threatened to beat his chest and grunt "Ooga-ooga" instead of saying "I do" at the proper moment. It wouldn't have seemed all that inappropriate if all the guests knew what I knew. For this was the wedding of the ape and the naked lady. I want you to know now there is a happy ending to this story.

For twenty years, I taught a year-long course called "Graphics" in a private high school. The students called the course "Art for Turkeys"—because it was designed for those who thought they had no artistic talent but wished otherwise. The course was a mix of learning to draw, history of art, philosophy of art, and, as it turned out, sex education.

In the spring of the year, the Graphics class spent six weeks drawing the human figure. Nude. Naked. Both *male* and *female*. The students knew, from the art-history lectures and visits to museums, that artists had considered the human form a worthy subject for thousands of years. And they, in becoming artists, might as well do likewise. To open the door to the mystery and see it literally in the light of day.

Besides, adolescents already have a very serious interest in the human body. And at the same time, a discomforting fear. You may remember. Your own body was developing, and all your friends' bodies were developing. And you had no control over this—it happened to you. Bodies were connected to sex. Probably the single thing you thought most about for at least ten years of your life.

We drew the nude human form in the Graphics class as an exercise in growing up—to suspend prejudice and lust and fear. To see what was truly amazing and beautiful about the human body—and to report that with the language of pencil and paint.

Despite what parents and faculty might think, this was no first unveiling of the secrets of secrets. The students were not ignorant or innocent. Every last one of them had at least seen *Playboy* and *Playgirl* magazines, and most of them had viewed R- and X-rated movies and videos. All had taken sex education and biology courses. If statistical surveys were accurate, many already were having sexual relations, and others would if they could.

These were late-twentieth-century teenagers. It was a mistake to underestimate what they knew. And an equal mistake not to ask them to go one more step and see the human body through the lens of art.

It wasn't so easy to convince parents and the school administration. But to make this long story short at this point, it is to the credit of the school that the matter was dealt with fairly and thoughtfully, and the drawing of the nude human figure became an integrated part of the Graphics course and the life of the school.

After a while, nobody thought much about it anymore. The event came and went without controversy for quite a few years. Samples of student work were placed on view or were taken home, and were received with murmurs of appropriate critical appreciation. No problem.

(The ape and the naked lady are coming now.)

It was a Friday. For a week we had been drawing the human figure by working from prints of famous paintings. Now it was time to consider the real thing. Our model was herself an artist and came to us from the nearby university, where she also posed for classes. She was young, attractive, auburn-haired, and shapely. Rubens would have approved.

An important part of what happened next involves the assistant headmaster of the school. Remember him?—back there at the faculty meeting knifing. Tall, handsome, serious, ambitious, bright, and eager to succeed at his job. He had come to us in the fall from a very traditional boys' school in Los Angeles, and had been left alone in charge of the school for the first time, while our headmaster was away at meetings.

He did not know that three floors directly above his head there was a naked woman. He would not have believed it. It never would have occurred to him. And I neglected to mention the model to him, because the fact of her existence in spring term had blended into the life of the school several years before he came.

Imagine him sitting at his desk, facing the door to his office, which opens onto the main hallway of the school. It is almost three o'clock and the end of the school day.

Just one more piece of information before the action really begins: The model had a boyfriend. Both the model and the boyfriend occasionally attended my church. I knew them socially. The boyfriend was coming to pick up the model at the end of the school day, and as long as he was there, he thought he might as well play a joke on me. He would rent an ape costume and kidnap the model.

There is quiet in the studio.
　Model is posing.
　Students are drawing.
　Mozart is on the stereo.
　All is well.

I leave the room for a little while to give the students a chance to work without my looking over their shoulders and to get some more supplies from a storeroom. While I am there, I hear cheering from the studio, then quiet again. I return to the studio. The class is gone. And so is the model. A prank, I suppose—they're just hiding somewhere. I'm cool. They will be back soon, of course.

What I don't know is that the boyfriend has charged into the room in his ape suit, beat his chest, hollered "OOGA-OOGA," picked up the naked lady in his arms, and charged off down the stairs.

The class thought it was me in the costume.

Cheering, they jumped up and chased down the stairs behind the ape. Three floors down to the main hall and then all the way down the hall from one end to the other and out the door at the other end, passing, you may remember, the open door of the assistant headmaster, who has bolted up out of his chair and stumbled to his doorway as the ape, naked lady, and students stormed down the hall and out the door. OOGA-OOGA!

Calmly, I walk down the stairs, looking for my class.

I know nothing about what's happened. Nothing. I swear.

And headed my way is the assistant headmaster, who is nonplussed and inarticulate. He thinks I have set him up. He also thinks it was me in the ape costume. But that can't be—here I am. He shouts, "What the HELL, Fulghum—what's with the APE and the NAKED LADY?"

The ape and the naked lady, in the meantime, have jumped into the ape's pickup truck and have driven away. The students have returned to the studio by another stairway.

The assistant headmaster pulls me by the arm out the front door.

"Out here."

But there's nothing out there but a driveway, some trees, and a lawn.

Years later. The assistant headmaster still thinks I did a number on him. The students still think it was me in the costume. And the ape married the naked lady, and they have a couple of little apes of their own now. "Ooga-ooga."

Is this story true? That's my version. The ape and the naked lady and the assistant headmaster, of course, have theirs. The varying truth perceived by many witnesses is a fact of life.

For example, let me add one final view of this ridiculous event, contained in a letter I received this past year from an alumna of the school—a student in that very Graphics class.

She confessed that she had been afraid to be in the same room with a mixed crowd and a nude model, and even more, she was afraid to be afraid. She didn't eat all day. She was a doubting Catholic, but she seriously prayed to God that some miracle would happen if she went to class. She arrived late—just as the ape carried the naked lady away. Her prayer had been answered. A miracle. God had provided an almost unbelievable solution.

She said it kept her going to church for a long time.

GRAND JUNCTION, COLORADO. HOT AFTERNOON in mid-July. Local newspaper headline says: POWER SHORTAGE IN GRAND JUNCTION.

In the men's room in the local airport passenger terminal, another kind of power problem is in progress. From behind a stall door comes the sharp cry of a small child: "No, no, no, no, no. I won't. I won't."

Followed by an imploring voice of a man under great pressure. "Please. Do it for Daddy?" and the little voice replies, "No. No, no, no, no, no."

The seven men using the facilities turn their faces in unison toward the stall with what-the-hell looks. In the opening at the bottom of the door, two sets of feet can be seen. A small pair, sockless, in black patent-leather sandals. And a much larger pair, in polished brown cowboy boots. The encounter continues:

"Look, I know you have to go. You go every day. If you don't go now, you'll have to go when we're standing in line or after we're strapped into our seats or when we're thirty-five-thousand feet in the air, and you'll probably mess your pants and we'll have to clean you up when we're way up there and you don't want to have to do that and I don't want to have to do that so why don't you just go now like a good girl?"

"No. This is the boys' place."

"I know, but Daddy can't go into the girls' room."

"No."

"What will Mommy and Grandma say when we get off the plane and you've messed your pants and you're crying and I'm mad? They won't be glad to see us."

"Yes, they will."

"We're going to miss our plane if you don't go now."

"I don't care."

"Am I going to have to spank you?"

"No."

"Then please, please, at least try."

"No."

"If you'll go, I'll buy you an ice cream."

"No."

"I'll buy you a present—you can pick it."

"No."

"I'll give you a dollar."

"No."

"Please try—just as a favor to Daddy."

"No."

The big voice gets tough. "Well bygod you've just got to do it, that's all there is to it. You're going to sit on this pot until something happens."

The sounds of struggle as the small feet disappear. "Noooooooooooooooo."

"You ... little ... you ... little ... Aw, hell."

The stall door swings open.

A five-year-old girl emerges in tears, her lips puckered in fierce refusal and her mind set in cement as she marches solemnly past the onlookers and out the door.

Her father follows. Big man in a black Stetson. Red-faced mad. Embarrassed. Defeated. Humiliated.

Nobody pushes him around. Nobody tells him "No." But his five-year-old girl-child has done it. And she has also not done her "business." And there's going to be trouble in the air and a fracas when they get to Denver. He storms out the door after the child, fit to be tied.

The impromptu Committee of Wise Men who have witnessed this drama and who remain behind in the sudden quiet of the men's john render their judgments.

"Sure glad I ain't in his shoes."

"Ought to take the big guy into the bar and buy him a drink."

"Women—don't know what's worse trouble, the little ones or the big ones."

"That kid's gonna 'splode at thirty-five-thousand feet."

A guy washing his hands speaks with the wisdom of Solomon.

"If it had been me, I'd have given her a banana split, a hundred dollars, all the presents she could carry, and a United States Savings Bond before I would have got on that plane with her."

Later, I saw the man and his child headed back to the men's room in a big hurry. The little girl's disposal system had settled the matter. Now she *had* to go. The last I saw of father and daughter they were sitting side by side in silence. Just the two of them in the otherwise empty departure lounge.

They missed the plane.

I wish I could have heard him when he called his wife to explain.

Father and daughter will survive this ordeal.

Time will turn it into family legend.

This is the kind of story a father will save to tell

about his daughter at the rehearsal dinner of her wedding. It will be funny, especially with the embellishments fathers are prone to make. It is she who will be embarrassed this time. But the father will make it clear, as fathers sometimes do, that he's proud of this independent-minded child—has always been—and the groom had better understand that he's marrying a strong woman who has been thinking for herself for a long time.

*T*HOUGH THE FORMAL STUDY OF MUSIC WAS NOT part of my education or family life, I have always wished otherwise—always yearned to speak the language and know the customs that would give me a passport to that land across the border separating an audience from the stage.

How I have wished to be able to play or even conduct—to be part of the orchestra somehow, and not forever confined to a seat in the audience!

In *All I Really Need to Know I Learned in Kindergarten*, I mentioned my respect for symphonic music. Beethoven's Ninth in particular. In my secret life, I fantasized that someday I would rent a hall, a symphony orchestra, and a great chorale—and personally conduct that giant piece of music while simultaneously playing the kettle-drum parts.

About a year after the publication of *Kindergarten*, I received an astonishing call from a representative of the Minneapolis Chamber Symphony. The fantasy in my book had been noted. Would I be interested in conducting at least the final movement of the Ninth? My presence would give them some useful public attention, and I could fulfill my dream. How about it?

I assumed they knew what they were doing, or they would not have asked.

They assumed I knew what I was doing, or I would not have written knowledgeably about Beethoven.

And I assumed that what I had always heard was true: that an orchestra really doesn't need a conductor. All you had to do was give the downbeat and gyrate your arms in time to the music all the way to the end and take a bow.

As for Beethoven and his Ninth Symphony, I had read the available literature and attended live performances of the piece. On many occasions I had conducted it—while standing alone in my living room.

Of course. I could do this.

On behalf of my new self-image as the Legendary Fuljumowski, I accepted.

And thereby set in motion a wave of extraordinary events. It will take a while to tell you, but as in a symphony, all the small parts are necessary for the whole.

There were not just a *few* things I did not know about what I had got myself into. For one thing, the orchestra was in turmoil—in one of those seasons of self-destructive chaos that arts organizations are prone to endure. Its founding conductor had been fired by its board. Key musicians had resigned in protest. A new conductor had not yet been hired. Despite the catharsis and purge, planning for the coming orchestral season was necessarily being carried forward by an office staff who knew a lot about promotion but not as much about me and Beethoven's Ninth as they should have.

By the time the new conductor arrived, the season had been announced. He and the orchestra were privately appalled to hear about me. The conductor came to visit me in Seattle, and with gentle forbearance he inquired:

"Just how well do you read an orchestral score, Mr. Fulghum?"

I replied, "I don't read music at all. Is that really a problem?"

There was a long pause in the conversation.

He explained that the Ninth was so difficult that most professional conductors wouldn't attempt it until they had years of experience.

He explained that in the final movement alone there were at least thirty-one places where the conductor had to stop and start the orchestra with sensitive changes in tempo.

He explained that a chamber orchestra did not normally include the Ninth in its repertoire, since they had only twenty-six musicians and must add players for big pieces. Not only would there be fifty musicians to lead, but there were a hundred members of the chorus to conduct, plus four soloists. Though they were all professional musicians, very few, if any, of the players or singers had ever performed the Ninth. Even if they could play and sing the music, getting the group to come together as a cohesive ensemble would be a major task.

He explained that while I was doing so well in my living room waving my arms, I was about a half-second behind the music and could leave and go to the bathroom and come back and they would still be playing. In the real concert setting, the conductor must have the complete score in his head. In the real concert hall, the conductor must be thinking seconds ahead, knowing everything that had happened, was presently happening, and was going to happen in the next minute—all at once.

He explained until he reached a mental impasse.

"In sum, what you want to do is . . . is . . . is . . . so . . . so . . . completely . . ."

He couldn't find the words.

"But I really, really want to do this," I pleaded.

Another long pause in the conversation.

He said, and I quote directly: "We are in deep shit."

He had found the right words, all right—he had finally come up with a formal musical term I could fully comprehend.

To his surprise, and even to my own, I was not dissuaded.

"But *could* it be done—I mean, if I worked hard enough and long enough and wanted to do this badly enough? Is it *possible*?"

"Maybe."

We made a deal. He would help me in every way he could to learn conducting in the most elemental way. Which proved a little easier than I expected, since clarity and simplicity and consistency were far more important than dramatics.

I promised to do something I had not done since high school: to learn something—in that wonderful phrase—*by heart*. To memorize the piece so thoroughly it would always be a part of me.

And to translate the score into some idiosyncratic form I could follow.

We would give it six months. If I could pull it off, well and good. If not, I promised to become catastrophically ill a week before the performance and not show up at all.

When I went to work on the Ninth, I fell back on my college skills. On that attitude that says there is no intellectual task that cannot be performed between noon on Sunday and a 9:00 A.M. Monday class, if that's what stands between you and passing a course. If you're worried enough and scared enough and desperate enough, you can do miraculous things with your mind.

Not only could you read *War and Peace* if you had to, you'd even consider writing a sequel to *War and Peace*. Thinking back on what I pulled off to get my B.A., Beethoven's Ninth seemed less daunting. It also helped my morale when I learned that the first time Beethoven conducted it in rehearsal, he crashed it—never got through it. Beethoven bombed.

Learning the Ninth may have been the hardest and most exciting intellectual challenge of my life. It was so impossibly absurd a thing to attempt I could not turn away. How bad could it be? The worst I could do was bring about a hilarious debacle nobody would ever forget. At best, I could actually do it.

This was a *must*. A crazy, unimaginable, no-way-out *must*.

One week before the concert, I presented myself to the maestro in a nervous-but-ready-as-I'll-ever-be condition. We worked daily. While he played through the score on the piano, he cajoled and shouted and sang me up and down the changes.

He never said it, but I believe to this day he knew I couldn't do it and he knew I knew I couldn't do it, but he would leave it to the disaster of the first rehearsal to speak the truth to me.

This man has a Yale Ph.D. and is a gentleman and a scholar. He also has a wicked sense of humor, so I also suspect he did not want to miss out on what promised to become one of the great comedy moments in recent symphonic history.

And speaking of truth, it was only at this stage that I learned about the distemper of the orchestra. The wounds of the war over the leadership and personnel changes in the orchestra were not healed. Contract negotiations between the union and the board had not been settled. And to top it off, the season would begin with the tacky idea of a chamber orchestra doing part of the Ninth with an amateur wannabe at the podium.

It was true—they didn't need a conductor.

What they needed was a minister.

I knew how to do that.

By looking at the orchestra through the lens of ministry, I saw the obvious—namely, that musicians appeared to be a great deal like people I knew well.

It's easy to be fooled. When you sit out there in a great concert hall and these handsome, beautiful, formally dressed, talented people walk purposefully onto the stage with their shining instruments, they seem like minor gods. Not a care in this world.

If you go to a closed rehearsal, where only the musicians are present, you will find a raggedy bunch of people not unlike those you see in a checkout line at a supermarket. They have come to work—to do their job—and go home. Since they are overworked and underpaid, you quickly learn that the beautiful black outfits you see from the audience are, upon closer examination backstage, likely to have been assembled from the local thrift shops.

They had children, wives, husbands, homes, hopes, dreams, and all the rest. All had committed their lives to the hardscrabble road of the professional musician at some sacrifice to the usual quality-of-life standards. They made sacrifices to make music. Anybody who was interested in their lives was welcome.

I learned that within the core group of the orchestra, there were a couple of divorces in progress, a mother dying of cancer, a family in financial crisis, some rivalries and jealousies, a drinking problem, and the tension of us-versus-them between the regular players and the extras hired to do the Ninth.

The orchestra wasn't feeling good about itself. The musicians' humanity was somewhat in disarray. So when this fool amateur conductor showed up and said "Teach me," "Help me," "Give me your best and I will give you mine," their mood changed from depression to amused distraction.

They needed respect, and great respect was surely mine to give.

First rehearsal.

I stood on the podium, raised my hands, and, with crazed confidence, gave a hopeful downbeat. And they played!

For the very same reasons that everything goes haywire at times, everything works sometimes. Like this time. It wasn't great—we stumbled and fumbled and lurched along, but we hung together and it was done. I couldn't believe it. The orchestra was amazed. The conductor was dumbfounded. And I was ready to pack up and go home. Once was enough, thank you very much. The thought of three more rehearsals and three performances left me limp.

The conductor, on the other hand, felt rejuvenated. What impressed him was my apparent lack of reliance on the score—I never looked at it. Yet I seemed to anticipate every entrance of every instrument. I was focused like I had radar working. He couldn't believe it.

"But that's nothing," I said. "If you watch them, just before they are about to play, they hold up their instruments in the ready position, and you just wave at them—COME ON IN—and they do. I thought you knew that."

He was always checking the score—he'd never noticed.

Professionals don't know everything.

* * *

Well, we came to the first performance. The World Theater in St. Paul, Minnesota—a full house. Whereas I had once looked forward to wearing the white tie and tails of a maestro, I now knew enough to know such dress would only compound the joke. Holding a baton was like holding a moon rock—a simple item that represented enormously complicated human capability. I now knew the truth of the statement that only 10 percent of conducting is conducting.

So I didn't look much like a conductor, dressed in a business suit as I was. And I didn't come from backstage, but from out of a seat in the second row of the audience. I explained to the audience that I represented them and anybody among them who had always wanted to conduct. I apologized for not carrying a conductor's baton. Every time I had used it in rehearsal, I had thrown it into the chorus.

I turned, stepped up onto the podium, inhaled enough oxygen to approach hyperventilation, and gave the downbeat. For better or worse, we were off. I felt the way a surfer must feel slicing along inside the curl of a mighty wave.

My problem was that every time we came to a change of tempo, I experienced an adrenaline rush and came in waving my arms at a speed about ten beats faster than normal. Once, at a place where we were supposed to go from a slow 60 two-beat to a fast three-beat, I whipped in at about ninety beats a minute—the upper limit for strings for a sustained passage. We were smoking. Moving like a runaway train. I told the orchestra later it was a powerful moment.

A *religious* moment.

Because I'm thinking, OHMYGOD, OHMYGOD, and I look down at the first cello madly sawing away, and she's looking across at the first violin, who is likewise pumping his fiddle for all he's worth, and she silently mouths "Ohmygod, ohmygod" at him.

The next day, one of our critics called the performance "crisp."

We had got through the Ninth in record time.

Truthfully appraised, the performance wasn't good or consistent or even competent. But I, the trained seal from Seattle, had balanced Beethoven's ball on my nose while clapping my hands in time to the music. For what it was, it was what it was, and what the people came to see: the Maestro Fuljumowski on a roll—leaving the audience feeling any one of them might have conducted at least as well.

Came the final night of a three-performance series, I was in trouble. I didn't think I could do it again. Drained, exhausted, and oversatisfied, I was also worried about the value of what I was trying to do. Just doing barely well enough to get through this thing was an insult to the greatness of the music and the talent of the musicians. Nobody had to tell me that. I knew. I remembered that most of the musicians had never done the Ninth before. This might be their only chance. And because of me, they would have done it only in a half-baked way. They might never know what it was like to do it at the top of their form. Now that I really knew what I was doing, how could I possibly do it? In the attic of my secret life, my committee was giving me a beating. Who did I think I was?

There was a larger consideration, too. Here we were in the World Theater about to do Beethoven, and in the theater of the world great dramas had recently taken place—events that called for this music to be played. The Berlin Wall had come down. Mandela had walked free. Democracy was brewing in China. We were about to play the music associated with great triumph—the "Ode to Joy"—played when barriers fell, when freedom came, and humanity touched glory for a moment. Music made out of Beethoven's defiance of his fate of deafness and old age.

I wondered how I could possibly go through with this ego trip of mine and stumble through the Ninth one more time. And yet, that's what we'd advertised, and that's what the people had bought tickets to see and hear. Right up to the very last moment, I didn't know what to do. How could I? How could I not?

The hall was packed. A black-tie evening. The orchestra and chorus filed onstage for one last go at this preposterous task. The lights dimmed in the hall. I climbed slowly up the stairs to the stage and stepped slowly up onto the conductor's podium, and turned, slowly, to the orchestra to ask the musicians for their attention as if we were ready to begin. I paused.

No. I couldn't do it.

In that expectant silence, I turned to the audience and told them of the struggle going on in my mind. I talked about Beethoven's great cry of "YES!" that was contained in this music, and about the sorrowful silence from which it roared.

I told them the story of Fulghum the wannabe conductor, who only now understood what he had got himself into. I told them about the real people who played in this orchestra. I spoke of the human triumphs going on in our time that paralleled the spirit of this music.

"I can't dishonor this man or this music or this spirit," I told them.

I asked the real conductor to come and do justice.

I turned to ask the musicians to give it their all. And when I turned back to the audience, they had replied to my unspoken request for their consent by spontaneously rising from their seats to stand and be as much a part of the music as they could. Everywhere in the hall the mood was yes.

The maestro lifted his baton, and Beethoven carried us away.

And me? Where was the ex-maestro while the music flowed forth?

Having never sung in the chorus on this thing, I thought I'd just go back and stand in with them. True, I don't know any more about German than I do about orchestral scores. So what? If I could conduct it, how hard could this be?

I sang.

It was the orchestra's finest night. The musicians were finally united. The chorus and soloists poured out a mighty sound. For a time, all of us in the hall could believe in the power of the human spirit to overcome evil. Beethoven lived. We lived. Nothing grander could be said or done at that moment in our lives. At the end, when that marbled music rumbled down the hill of the heart like a landslide, people cheered their lungs out, pounded their hands together, hugged each other, threw flowers, and wept. What a night—what a world—what a life! YES!

I HAVE SET A BAD EXAMPLE MORE THAN ONCE IN MY life.

In at least one instance, I am pleased to have done so.

For several years I ran a fairly regular route for exercise, every other day. I actually don't run much anymore. At my age, running hard easily leads to knee, ankle, hip, and back damage—chronic problems that could interfere with dancing.

Dancing has priority.

Fortunately, I live at the bottom of a great hill. So now I march up that hill, trot a little, walk my route, and go down and back up and down several long stairways to get the blood pumping for an hour.

There was a time when my goal was to cover this three-mile route as quickly as possible. I carried a stopwatch. Focused on getting through each section just a little faster each day. Getting in shape as quickly as possible was the goal. Time and distance were the measuring rods of a successful morning. Just do it and do it and do it—better and better every day.

A stranger changed all that.

A woman whose schedule seemed to coincide with mine. She was usually somewhere on my route at the same time I was. We nodded. I was in a hurry. She was not.

A slim, gray-haired woman about my age, who wore comfortable clothes and high-tech walking shoes. She caught my eye for two reasons—she followed an erratic course, and she carried a plastic shopping bag. I wondered why.

When I stopped running and started walking, I had time to observe her more carefully. Over a couple of weeks, I put her route together as I saw her here and there. Though she marched along at a brisk pace, she always stopped to pick up trash and put it in her bag. She didn't make a big deal out of it or go out of her way—just tended to her own path, cleaned up the world under her own feet.

Her route zigzagged uphill a block and then went level for a block and then uphill again. At the top, she sat briefly on a park bench to admire the morning sky and the mountains to the east.

Next she looped through the cemetery, around a great redwood tree, pausing to read names on tombstones.

Then across a children's playground going up a ladder and down a slide, followed by a swing through the monkey bars.

Next through a scattered grove of tall fir trees, up the stairs to the top of a water tower, around a pond where she stopped to admire the water lilies, along an alley where she looked over a fence and into a greenhouse. Out into the park again to an open field of grass where she lay down on her back for a short time.

Then down to the Episcopal cathedral—inside briefly—and out again.

In one door of the art school next door, down a hall, and out a door at the other end of the building.

Down three long flights of stairs, under the freeway, and down to the local bakery for a cinnamon roll and cup of coffee.

One morning I joined her at her table at the bakery and introduced myself, explaining that we seemed to share the same exercise route, though I noticed she added some unexpected detours to hers.

She knew who I was, and she had also been aware of me—"the man in a hurry." To my surprise, she had been influenced by me, seeing in my morning rush a model for the kind of life she was living but hated. She had decided not to be like me.

The woman is a family doctor.

For years she had rushed off every morning to make rounds at the hospital and make healthful suggestions to patients that she did not act on in her own life.

She began to notice death and how fast she was running to meet hers.

"Haste does not improve the quality or quantity of life, you know," she advised me. So I had heard.

She decided not only to tend to her physical health, but the health of her mind and soul. "I lost touch with me, somehow," she said.

Not being a religious type or interested in cults or fads or isms, she decided that common sense would suffice for devising a new morning routine. No big conversion—no big deal—just *think, then do*.

To add usefulness to self-concern, she would pick up trash along her route—not try to clean up the whole neighborhood, mind you, but to do her share as she came to it.

To learn to see something new, she would go at least one block out of her way each morning as a very small adventure away from efficiency and into curiosity. That's how she found the greenhouse in an alley, the cemetery, several great trees, a garden dedicated entirely to edible plants, and the children's playground.

It was hard for her to explain the stop at the Episcopal cathedral. She wasn't religious, yet there was something important about standing alone in a great room set aside to mark a relationship with the Eternal.

The art school next door to the cathedral always had a show of student work in the front hall, and she liked being near evidence of a continuing struggle for creative expression, so she always walked down that hall slowly.

What amazed her in all this was the closeness of delightful things that she had missed for so long because she was in a hurry and focused on efficient exercise.

She explained, "I think of my morning adventure as going to get the news of the day. It's not all on the radio or in the paper, you know."

"And don't forget your part in this—it was because I didn't want to be like you that I found another way."

We serve our fellow men—and women—unexpectedly.

Even by being a bad example.

ONE OF THE WISEST MEN I KNOW, ALEXANDER Papaderos, is the director of the Orthodox Academy of Crete. Unfortunately for me, he lives ten time zones and thousands of miles away from Seattle. Even when we are together, we are separated by the subtleties of language. His English is far better than my Greek, but we both are seriously limited by lack of common cultural experience. We get by in English on most mundane topics, but when we reach for deeper understandings, we must be careful, lest we assume we are communicating when in fact we are not.

As 1992 became 1993, we spent the New Year holidays together. For all the romantic images a summer trip to Greece may suggest, the island of Crete in winter is a cold, windy, rainy place. A time to sit indoors by an olive-wood fire, drink raki and retsina, eat pork sausage with fresh bread soaked in new-pressed olive oil, and talk late into the night of weighty matters.

One evening we spoke of marriage.

In Crete the custom of arranged marriage continues. Even when a marriage is not initiated by a family, the wisdom of family experience is brought to bear in a way Americans would find anachronistic.

The Cretans think romance is nice enough when it happens, but it is not a particularly good basis for marriage.

Papaderos had stumbled over a concept he had found in Western literature. "Making love." It confused him. "What is this making love?"

I explained that it was a popular euphemism for having sex—going to bed, getting laid—whether married or not.

He replied that for Cretans, "making love" is a serious notion summarizing the process of marriage and family. When two families agree that a son and a daughter would suit one another, it is expected that over time the man and woman will work at becoming compatible partners in the same spirit one might work at achieving competence in a life's vocation. This is making love.

Time and experience—mistakes and difficulties—are all part of the equation whose sum is a lasting relationship. Love is not something you fall into. Love and marriage are "made."

Thus, in Cretan terms, when a married couple have been overheard arguing or fighting, the Cretans smile knowingly and say, "Ah, they are making love."

During this same winter trip, Papaderos took my wife and me along as guests in the home of a Greek family on New Year's Day. Though I hate to admit it, I am a closet football fan, and this was the first time in memory I could not be spending the day watching representatives of American universities struggle to resolve the great human crisis of who is Number One. Nor would I be in touch with the professional-football run-up to the Super Bowl. I was vaguely anxious.

My youth and early manhood were permanently affected by Vince Lombardi, the coach of the legendary Green Bay Packers football team. Lombardi was about winning. Fair and square and by the rules—but winning. Winners worked harder and smarter. Winners were never wimps—when knocked down, they got up again. Winners played tough in the face of adversity, injury, and pain. Winners played hurt.

* * *

These thoughts floated in my mind as I coped with the unfamiliar traditions of a Creatan New Year meal. The old customs of the mountain villages prevailed. Instead of the Anglo-American whole roasted pig with an apple in its mouth, the Cretans celebrate with boiled sheep's heads. Yes.

Skinned, simmered, and served with eyeballs intact, the head is split, and the brains are scooped out with a spoon. The tongues are sliced and eaten like pâté. These delicacies are savored by the grandparents and other senior members of the family, but not by the younger generation of Greeks.

I watched the grandmother as she ate.

Eighty-eight years old. Blind in one eye, deaf in one ear, and shriveled by time and a hard life. She helped herself to each dish as it passed her way. She ate carefully, thoughtfully, and with undisguised pleasure.

I knew that she had survived mountain life, two world wars, the Greek civil war, and the repressions of the Dictatorship of the Colonels in the 1970s. Her husband was taken into the army. She did not hear from him for almost seven years. Her village was leveled by the Nazis, and she was imprisoned and beaten. For two years she had lived in caves, eating roots and rabbits to stay alive. No home, no job, no income, no medical care or insurance, no retirement plan or Social Security. She had lived without electricity, running water, even without fire at times in her life.

At the end of the meal, she challenged the "children" at the other end of the table to a singing contest. The "children" were men and women of middle age—her nieces and nephews, cousins, and in-laws. She and her equally ancient husband began the keening drone of a Cretan mountain song. It works like this: The challenger makes up a four-line rhyming verse, then everyone sings the common chorus, then someone from the opposing team makes up a four-line verse responding to the verse of the challenger, and again the chorus, and so on. It's a can-you-top-this contest in song. Extemporaneous and fast, it ends when one team or another cannot come up with the verse without missing a beat. Not easy.

The old lady sang her opponents into exhaustion. She literally left them speechless. Her last verse contained a hope that this coming year would be even better than the last, and who knows, if the rest of them lived as well as she, they might be able to keep up with her in a singing contest, though she doubted it. They doubted it, too. And so did I.

Never mind the bowl games. This New Year's Day I had seen a winner.

If Lombardi had a backfield with her kind of

stuff, the Green Bay Packers would still be winning. The lady was a champ. A winner of a lifetime contest. She had faithfully played her part despite injuries and sorrows.

She played hurt—every day of her life.

Football is only a game.

When the dinner was over, the old lady went into the kitchen, insisting on helping with the dishes. She came to the kitchen door with a bag of garbage and barked at her husband of sixty years. He groaned up out of his chair to do his duty, and she barked at him some more and he groaned back some more.

"What's going on?" I asked Papaderos.

"It seems her husband did not eat all of his salad and was singing off-key," he explained. "They are still making love—it takes forever."

I MET A MAN WHO LIVES IN A KIND OF EXISTENTIAL angst. He is obsessed with television news programs. This version of the news of the world convinces him the end of the world is coming.

However, he is confused at the moment. There's some good news lately. And he was convinced an event called the "Harmonic Convergence" was going to bring life as we know it to a halt. Five years ago, on August 16, 1987, the materialistic world was to have self-destructed. Taking a cue from a cycle of the Mayan calendar, an alignment of nine planets in the solar system, Aztec and Hopi and Cherokee prophecies, and the intuition of several important contemporary spiritual gurus, the prediction had been made. Several hundred thousand people believed it—great gatherings were held at important "power centers" in the western United States.

The motto of that cosmic event was, "When the light hits, the dark gets tough." I don't quite get it, but apparently a lot of people did.

The Harmonic Convergence signaled a five-year period of disaster, along with the collapse of industrial civilization. By now the worst should have happened. He was kind of looking forward to it.

He's stuck now. Disappointed. The end has not come. He doesn't know which way to turn or what to do. He wasn't prepared for things to start looking up.

But suppose—just suppose—he is indeed in tune with Harmonic Convergence and the Great Conclusion—he and all the other doomsday sayers?

When I consider such a thing, I think of Lot's wife.

Remember? In the Bible. Genesis, Chapter 19.

Jehovah decided to destroy the cities of Sodom and Gomorrah for their wicked ways. End of their world. But he spared the life of a man named Lot, his wife, and two daughters. They were good folks. Jehovah told them to run for their lives to the mountains and, above all, "Do Not Look Back."

As they ran for it, Lot's wife paused and looked back, anyhow.

We don't know her name. We only know what she did. She looked back.

And Jehovah punished her by turning her into a pillar of salt.

Now I've known that story since I was a kid, and I didn't understand it then and I don't understand it now and I don't know anybody who does. Or I should say, I don't understand the part about Jehovah turning her into a pillar of salt for looking back. What I do understand is her looking back. I would have looked back, too.

My guess is many of us would have turned around to see where we came from for the same reasons—curiosity, nostalgia, and compassion. And above all, regret. How sad that the only way for Jehovah to handle human failure was by unredeeming destruction. The Deity doesn't come off too well here or set much of an example, frankly.

But there's truth here.

Science confirms the spirit of this story. Sure enough, some fine day this planet will fall into the sun and be no more. Every last thing we've done, are doing, and will do—extinguished. Kaput. Finished.

The same is true for us as individuals—one day all of us will cease to be.

But to run from the inevitable isn't always our

way. To turn, out of our own free will, and face the facts as a matter of human curiosity, and as a matter of connection with all that lives—good and bad—*that* is more often our way.

I do not know her name, but Lot's wife is a relative of mine.

And "Ye are the salt of the earth" is a compliment.

WE HAVE LIVED ON A HOUSEBOAT FOR SEVERAL years, my wife and I, which may sound like a romantically bohemian style of life to some. Up close it might seem more realistically as though we are living in a floating (or sinking) slum.

This aquatic trailer court makes for tight community. Our lives overlap. This is village life. And we are literally connected to one another in that we share the same fragile water lines and power lines, and the same eccentric sewer system, and are moored to the same wobbly pilings. We haul our garbage to the same Dumpster at the head of the dock. Any breakdown in what comes or goes quickly affects us all. And the breakdowns make for some hilarious middle-of-the-night fire drills of the run-and-shout-and-mill-about variety. This closeness also means that we hear and see much of what goes on inside our houses and inside our families.

Why would people want to live like this? We, too, wonder that at times. You do have to have an unconventional view of housing requirements, I admit. And you don't get into this by accident. It's a very deliberate choice and a deliberate way to live.

It has its advantages, however. Help and company are always close by. The milk or beer or wine or bread you forgot at the store is always available next door. Tools and parts are handy, as is advice. In August, it's like going away to adult summer camp—only you're at home.

This floating village life appeals to me. I like living up close to these people. I compare my life to theirs. I learn from them and am enriched by gifts they never realize they give.

Like sunlight tea, for instance.

The lady next door is a nurse-practitioner, a very high order of professional nurse. Her specialty is oncology—working with cancer patients. She knows a lot about death and dying. She leads an intensely busy life. Works part time and goes to school part time, raises two small children and a husband in the small space of a houseboat. On the dock she maintains a flower garden in boxes and pots, and ashore she has a serious vegetable garden. It's exhausting at times to observe the pace of her life. I avoid watching her when she's in high gear.

Despite her busyness, in the summer she makes sunlight tea.

Tea the slow way.

In a clear gallon jar filled with cold water, she hangs small bags of tea and spices. Early in the morning, just before she leaves for work, the jar is placed out on the deck on a white metal table. Leaving the sun to make tea.

When she returns in the late afternoon, she pours out a glass of sunlight tea, adds ice, a lemon wedge, and mint from her garden. She sits down in a chair in the shade of an umbrella to enjoy summer in a glass.

We've never talked about this.

Sometimes I am home during the day in summer, working out on my deck. I keep an eye on her tea project. I note the color change from light yellow to deep amber. I think about all the energy being poured into the liquid. I think about the acknowledgment of time and energy. It calms me, slows me down, diminishes the haste of my life.

I confess that on more than one occasion I have gone over and helped myself to a glass, carefully topping off the jar with fresh water. Once I left dandelion flowers in the tea, but she never said a word. Some very fine parts of friendship don't have to be discussed.

* * *

Recently, I tried making moonlight tea.

It worked!

Now I'm thinking about winter starlight tea and tea from an eclipse.

The light from a meteor shower or a comet ought to make a great brew.

My wife says I get carried away by these things.

Exactly.

*I*T'S FUNNY THE TRICKS THE MIND PLAYS. THE longer I have mine, the less I understand how it works. Driving home from the office one night in June, I began humming the "Ode to Joy" theme from the last movement of Beethoven's Ninth Symphony. What triggers these sudden musical interludes?

I was also surprised that I didn't start thinking about my conducting experience in Minneapolis. What did come to mind was what happened the next week. It's a kind of coda—a separate passage that brings a larger composition to a close.

Even though the orchestra was not going to repeat the Ninth after the World Theater performances, I was so reluctant to part company with its members that I went along on a bus tour with them the next week. They were to combine a performance with a teaching session in a town way out on the flat western prairie of Minnesota.

We arrived in Marshall, Minnesota, on a cold afternoon in February, with light snow falling. The session was held in a junior high school orchestra room. If you closed your eyes and relied on your nose and ears, you would know you were in a junior high school. The slightly rancid smell of sweaty puberty and the sound of voices in transition from soprano to alto would give you the clues, and one glance at the string section alone would confirm where you were. Skinny little boys coping with cellos that outweighed them, and tall, gangly girl violinists adjusting hairdos during rests in the music.

The professional musicians sat side by side with the students in each section of the orchestra. Together they played a simple piece of music the students had been working on for weeks. As the snow and wind blew outside the window, an unbelievably poignant sound filled the room. Combining the true notes of those who devote their lives to making beautiful music with the wavering, dissonant notes made by those who were nervous almost beyond bearing to be sitting beside someone who could really play and would notice their inadequacy.

The students need not have worried. The professionals had been there in the beginner chairs themselves. They knew—they remembered. Now, they could help.

The joy of being an accomplished musician and playing in a professional orchestra is not found only during black-tie nights on the concert stage. Their patient, hand-holding persistence carried the students on when they faltered. The music rose and fell in waves of success and failure. Whatever the music lacked, it was played from the heart.

That night at the performance hall, I didn't have any responsibilities. So I spent backstage time being part music student and part orchestra chaplain—asking about instruments and listening to people talk. When it was time to go onstage, it seemed natural to me to go along. I just picked up a chair and walked out with them, sitting in the symphony without an instrument while they played. I had finally become what I most wanted to be—part of the orchestra. I played me.

On the long way back home in the bus, we sang and drank far too much beer, and they told orchestra jokes. We confessed all that had gone before our coming together to do the Ninth—the fear, the confusion, and the embarrassment. We toasted the dreams of those who reach for a piece of the glory—Beethoven, the junior high students of Marshall, Minnesota, and all of us, as well.

I told them my cup runneth over. I asked them please not to forget me, as I would not forget them. I asked them to keep me and my kind in mind when they played. And to never forget that music is much too important to be left entirely in the hands of professionals.

If you ever could attend a performance of the Minneapolis Chamber Symphony when it plays out in the small towns of rural Minnesota, you might notice an empty chair just to the right of the double bass player and just behind the violas. The orchestra voted to put it there permanently. The chair is for those who always wanted to be part of the symphony—not just as listeners, but among those upon whom the making of music depends. It is the chair in honor of all those who, however competently, embrace the impossible. Sit in that chair someday.

*H*ERE I WAS IN ATLANTIC CITY. AT MR. TRUMP'S Taj Mahal. Largest gambling casino in the world. Please understand I came to speak to a convention, not to gamble. Being a rational man, it is clear to me that gambling is ultimately a losing proposition—my interest is one of intellectual curiosity—about the sociological, anthropological, and economic dimensions of risk strategy and its consequences.

Do you believe that? Don't.

While I am walking around the casino floor—just looking around—the Devil is talking in my ear: "Take a chance—could be your lucky day—somebody wins, why not you?"

Right. Why not me? I've had conversations with the Devil on this subject before. Usually at racetracks. And it's always the same. Some fools win—why not me? I'd sure as hell like to know why not me.

The Devil continues. "Come on—just drop one dollar, one lousy dollar, in this machine right here—the one dollar they gave you compliments of the house—what can you lose?"

OK. One dollar.

Chinkety, chinkety, chinkety, chink. KAFOOM! Flashing lights, bells, sirens, and $264 is mine. And I am in league with the Devil again.

Nothing, absolutely nothing, like winning. Nothing like feeling lucky. Yes!

The roaming cashier rushes up to pay me, shouting "HERE'S A WINNER!"

And the people playing slot machines all around me flash envious smiles.

It's my lucky day.

Just then a man walks up to me and says he's a gambler—a craps shooter—and he thinks luck rubs off on people, and he's seen me hit the jackpot on this machine, and would I come over and just stand by him while he shoots craps, and if I do and he wins, he'll give me 10 percent of his take, and if he loses, it's no hard feelings, all right—all I have to do is to blow on his hand when he's holding the dice just before he throws, OK?

Of course it's OK. He's talking to Mr. Lucky now.

So he shakes 'em. I blows on 'em. He throws

'em, screaming "COME ON, BABY! COME ON, BABY!"

And *BAM!* He hits.

Shake, blow, throw, and *BAM!*—shake, blow, throw, and *BAM!*—he hits and hits. Nine, count'em, nine, straight times he gets his point.

By now a crowd has collected, betting on this guy's unbearably sweet luck, making side bets, yelling, whooping, screaming "COME ON, BABY!" because this guy never takes his winnings off the table—everything rides—and he's beating the odds to pieces. Sic 'em, dawg!

Tall blond lady next to me is rhythmically chanting softly to herself, "Ohmygod, ohmygod, ohmygod."

What exquisite madness it is to be around this kind of success—this defiance of the laws of luck. It can't be done, and this guy is doing it. Out on the high wire of fate, thumbing his nose at the ground-suck of gambling gravity. "COME ON, BABY!"

The guy pauses. "Nine is my lucky number," he says. And scooping up his chips, filling his pockets, he bows to the croupier and walks off a winner—to the cheers and applause of the limply ecstatic crowd. Whooha, in spades! What a guy!

What holds this story fast in my mind is not the excitement or the luck or all the money or the fact that he won. If he'd lost, he would have laughed it off.

I privately believe that any fool can be a good loser.

But that he quit when he was *that* far ahead— *that* I'll never forget.

To be a winner is great. To be a great winner— that's strong work.

Money talks, but it doesn't sing—luck does.

And only a few who dance with Lady Luck have *all* the moves.

P.S. Yes, he did give me my 10 percent. He did have *all* the moves.

WITHIN MY SECRET LIFE, THERE ARE TOUCH-stones. Ideas, phrases, facts, and notions I refer to time and time again—as often as I would consult a map when traveling. Among these treasures is a story from the world of chess.

I'm told that during an international competition many years ago, a man named Frank Marshall made what is often called the most beautiful move ever made on a chessboard. In a crucial game in which he was evenly matched with a Russian master player, Marshall found his queen under serious attack. There were several avenues of escape, and since the queen is the most important offensive player, the spectators assumed Marshall would observe convention and move his queen to safety.

Deep in thought, Marshall used all the time available to him to consider the board conditions. He picked up his queen—paused—and placed it down on the most illogical square of all—a square from which the queen could be captured by any one of three hostile pieces.

Marshall had sacrificed his queen—an unthinkable move, to be made only in the most desperate of circumstances.

The spectators and Marshall's opponent were dismayed.

Then the Russian and the crowd realized that Marshall had actually made a brilliant move. It was clear that no matter how the queen was taken, his opponent would soon be in a losing position. Seeing the inevitable defeat, the Russian conceded the game.

When the spectators recovered from the shock of Marshall's daring, they showered the chessboard with money. Marshall had achieved victory in a rare and daring fashion—he had won by sacrificing his queen.

To me it's not important that he won.

Not even important that he actually made the queen-sacrifice move.

What counts is that Marshall had suspended

standard thinking long enough even to entertain the possibility of such a move.

Marshall had looked outside the traditional and orthodox patterns of play and had been willing to consider an imaginative risk on the basis of his judgment and his judgment alone. No matter how the game ended, Marshall was the ultimate winner.

I've told that story countless times.

And on the checklist of operating instructions for my life, this phrase appears:

"Time to sacrifice the queen?"

It turns up in unexpected situations.

Now hold that thought while I pull out a childhood reference from my touchstone collection. Remember Tinkertoys? Interconnecting wooden parts—spools and rods—that came in tall canisters. Still do, but the parts are all plastic now.

When I taught art, I used Tinkertoys in a test at the beginning of a term. I wanted to know something about the creative instincts of my students. On a Monday, I would put out a small set of Tinkertoys in front of each student. And give a deliberately brief and ambiguous assignment: "Make something out of the Tinkertoys—you have forty-five minutes today and forty-five minutes each day for the rest of the week."

* * *

A few students were derailed at first. They were hesitant to plunge in. The task seemed frivolous. They wanted to know more about what I wanted and waited to see what the rest of the class would do.

Several others checked the instructions in the can and made something according to one of the sample model plans provided.

Another group built something out of their own imaginations or worked at finding how high or how long a construction they could devise.

Almost always at least one student would break free of the constraints of the set and incorporate pencils, paper clips, string, notebook paper, and any other object lying around the art studio—sometimes even leaving the class for a time to gather up soda straws from the cafeteria or small dry branches and sticks from the schoolyard. And once I had a student who worked experimentally with Tinkertoys whenever he had free time. His constructions filled a storeroom in the art studio and a good part of his basement at home.

I rejoiced at the presence of such a student.

Here was an exceptionally creative mind at work.

He had something to teach me.

His presence meant that I had an unexpected teaching assistant in class whose creativity would infect other students. I thought of him and other such students as "queen sacrificers." They had "Q-S"

This "Q-S" trait applies to almost any situation—even trivial ones. I came across one such student who had volunteered in the school alumni office to help with the mailing of a fund-raising appeal to major donors. His job was to place stamps on the envelopes. In true form, he was *not* licking the stamps and pasting them to the envelopes. He was *licking the envelopes* at just the right spot, then sticking a stamp on that spot. Pounding the stamp once with his fist, he moved on.

He explained that the adhesive on the stamps tasted awful. The envelopes, on the other hand, had an interesting cinnamon taste. And besides, the stamps stuck better this way.

Affirming this kind of thinking had a downside.

I ran the risk of losing those students who had a different style of thinking.

Without fail one would declare, "But I'm just not creative."

"Do you dream at night when you're asleep?"

"Oh, sure."

"So tell me one of your most interesting dreams."

Invariably the student would spin out something wildly imaginative.

Flying or on another planet or in a time machine or growing three heads.

"That's pretty creative. Who does that for you?"

"Nobody. I do it."

"Really—at night, when you're asleep?"

"Sure."

"Try doing it in the daytime, in class, OK?"

One more touchstone now and this puzzle will fit together.

On a hot summer's day, late in August, I sought shade and a cool drink under the canvas awning of a waterfront café in the old harbor of the town of Chania, on the Greek island of Crete. More than 100 degrees in still air. Crowded. Tempers of both the tourists and waiters had risen to meet the circumstances, creating a tensely quarrelsome environment.

At the table next to mine sat an attractive young couple. Well dressed in summer fashions of rumpled linen and fine leather sandals. The man: stocky, olive-complexioned, black hair, and mustache. The woman: lanky, fair, blond. Waiting for service, they held hands, whispered affections, kissed, giggled, and laughed.

Suddenly, they stood, picked up their metal table, and, carrying it with them, stepped together off the edge of the quay to place the table in the shallow water of the harbor. The man waded back for the two chairs. He gallantly seated his lady in the waist-high water and sat down himself.

The onlookers laughed, applauded, and cheered.

A sour-faced waiter appeared. He paused for the briefest moment. Raised his eyebrows. Picked up a tablecloth, napkins, and silverware. Waded into the water to set the table and take their order. Waded back ashore to the ongoing cheers and applause of the rest of his customers. Minutes later he returned with a tray carrying a bucket of iced champagne and two glasses. Without pausing, he waded once more into the water to serve the champagne. The couple toasted each other, the waiter, and the crowd. And the crowd replied by cheering and throwing flowers from the table decorations.

Three other tables joined in to have lunch in the sea.
    The atmosphere shifted from frustration to festival.
    One does not wade into the water in one's best summer outfit. Why not?
    Customers are not served in the sea. Why not?
    Sometimes one should consider crossing the line of convention.
    One need not be in a classroom or playing chess.
    Whenever life becomes Tinkertoys, the queen may be sacrificed.

A FRIEND FROM ALGERIA WILL NOT EAT PORK. HE grew up in an Islamic culture where pork was considered unclean. Though he has lived in the United States for several years, and though he no longer practices the religion of his childhood, he still does not eat pork in any form. In part of his mind, he knows about the history of food taboos, and he knows that millions of people eat pork all the time with no harmful effects. Still, for him, for reasons he cannot articulate, pork is unclean.

To give me some perspective on how he feels, he sent me a newspaper article stating that "200,000 Taiwanese are drinking their own urine daily. Their purpose is to cure disease, improve health, and achieve longevity."

The story concerned a man named Chen Ching Chuan, who was applying for a new identity card in Taiwan a couple of years ago. The police thought he was lying to them because he looked about thirty-five or forty years old, though he was actually sixty-four. When he attributed his youthful appearance to the fact that he had been drinking his own urine, the story was picked up by the reporter covering the police station and became international news. Upon investigation, reporters found that Mr. Chen Ching Chuan does indeed drink three cups of his own urine every day. Moreover, he says that morning urine is best.

I am not making this up.

Mr. Chen Ching Chuan has become so well known and so many people are following his example that he has set up a urine-therapy hot line to provide advice on this matter. Also, you can buy a book entitled *The Golden Water Cure*, which documents cases in which seriously ill patients have regained their health through urine therapy.

Those who have reason to know say urine from a healthy person tastes like beer, when served cold. Mr. Chen Ching Chuan notes that "urine, like blood, is full of nutrition; therefore drink all of it and don't waste a drop. What happens when you regularly drink urine is beyond your imagination."

Trying to be objective about all this, I consulted

a friend of long standing, whose integrity, intelligence, and professional experience qualify him as an expert on the subject of urine. He is a urologist, who has spent time in both clinical and research medicine.

He said he doesn't think urine therapy is going to catch on, but it is true that drinking normal urine won't hurt you, and given the mysteries of the placebo effect, it's likely to be as useful as any other substance that provokes the body's capacity to care for itself. He went on to say that urine has prevented death by dehydration in extreme crisis situations. It's free and readily available. And, yes, as a matter of fact, he has tasted it. And, yes, it does taste like beer—warm or cold.

Further research turned up a book widely distributed in India, under the auspices of Morarji Desai, who has held many high positions in government, including that of prime minister. The book is *Mana Mootra* ["human urine"]; *The Elixir of Life*. It's full of documentation by Western-trained physicians and scientists who confirm the value of drinking urine daily. Apparently, millions of Indians do. Mr. Desai feels so strongly about this matter that he would like to make urine therapy a mandated part of government policy.

Now we're into serious politics. Can you imagine the campaign rhetoric in our own country? "My party's national health plan is for everyone to drink a glass of urine first thing every morning."

Maybe it would go over. I mean, if we can survive on generous helpings of horse manure as government policy, who is to say human urine isn't a reasonable alternative?

Thinking of urine brings to mind time spent in a doctor's office waiting room. Waiting, and waiting. With little to do except read old magazines and watch other patients as they watch me. Every once in a while a person's name is called, and that person goes up to the desk to consult with the nurse and then shuffle down the hall to the rest room.

Whether man or woman, when they come out, they act furtively, as if they've done something they should not have done. They glance around to see if anybody is watching. Quickly, they put a little jar on the nurse's desk and hastily return to their seat to begin intensely reading a tattered copy of a 1975 edition of *Woman's Day*.

What they left up there on the desk was a urine sample.

Everybody's done it. Remember the first time?

"Do what? In this? How? What the hell for?"

It's something nice people do only for the sake of medical science. If you weren't sick or you weren't cowed by doctors and nurses, you wouldn't do this—not even alone in your bathroom at home.

An average person excretes more than fifty thousand quarts of urine in an average lifetime. Odd that something all of us so regularly manufacture—something so necessary and useful—should have such negative connotations.

Urine is unclean. Period.

But the facts of the matter contradict this position.

Every respectable source I've consulted confirms that urine isn't dirty.

Fresh urine is cleaner than saliva.

Urine is cleaner than your hands are most of the time, cleaner than your bacteria-infested toothbrush, and freer of germs than the tuna-fish sandwich you ate for lunch. These items are crawling with bad stuff.

Not urine. Urine has no bacteria in it.

It's 95 percent water and 5 percent urea, which is what's left after proteins break down.

It contains traces of about two hundred minerals and compounds, including ammonia, calcium, magnesium, sodium, and potassium.

It's useful, too.

You can tan leather with it and use it as a fertilizer. Also as a dye and a detergent. It will clean your hair.

If you are dying of thirst, it will prolong your life.

I don't know why it's yellow instead of red or blue or green. Two physiologists and a urologist couldn't tell me. It was too simple a question.

I do know that we all make about two quarts a day and that it's legal, moral, necessary, and generally OK to do so. If you don't, you die.

And I repeat. No matter what you were taught—no matter what you think, even after all this—urine really isn't dirty.

So. Does that mean I'm going to start drinking mine?

No way.

*H*ERE COMES A FISH STORY. A TRUE FISH STORY. There are three very reliable witnesses. They will be embarrassed to confirm these facts, for they are *serious* fishermen—and maybe I'm not.

My main fishing experience consists of stock-tank fishing, Texas style. In a ranch pond primarily used to water cattle, fingerling fish are planted. When you want to have a fish fry, you throw a lighted stick of dynamite out into the pond. *KAFOOM!!* Whatever floats up gets cooked. If you don't want too many fish, you stick the wire leads of an old hand-crank telephone in the water and crank until you electrocute one or two fish. This is fishing at its efficient best—fast and cheap, with minimal equipment, fuss and bother. Exciting, too.

One summer my friend Willy, his nine-year-old son, David, and Gen, my nine-year-old nephew visiting from Japan, were primed to assault the mighty rainbow trout high in the Cascade Mountains in a remote lake "absolutely full of fish"—a record catch was promised. Would I come? How could I not? I had never been fishing the way gentlemen do it. It was time.

The license I received is still in my scrapbook. I had no idea how official fishing could get. License number 890046566, issued August 3, 1989, at 9:30 A.M. In addition to my address, I had to list my date of birth, citizenship, years of residency in the state, my sex, height, weight, and color of eyes. For seven dollars, I was allowed three consecutive days of fishing. On the dotted line where it states that "I certify, under penalty of law, that the above information is true, and I agree to show license and game to wildlife agent when requested," I signed my name. I won't quote the small print on the back of the license, but I don't think I did or caught or shot or mutilated any of the items listed. Obtaining the license was a sobering experience. Someone told me it's easier to get a handgun than a fishing license.

By myself I visited a local sporting-goods store, explaining that I knew nothing about fishing but must be properly equipped since I did not want to humiliate my nephew and dishonor the family name by appearing inept, ignorant, or underequipped.

How the clerk appreciated having somebody like me walk into his store!

How pleased he was to educate and equip me.

How grateful I am that we were only out to catch fish and not kill rhinosceri.

He appreciated me $280 worth. But I felt good going out of that store with my gear. I knew now that only 10 percent of fishing is fishing—the rest is gear. And I felt ready. Let the safari commence. Let the fish beware. Bring on the tenacious trout!

With full camping kit, we four marched into the mountains to the "lake full of fish," set up our tents, talked of how many fish we could eat, and went to bed.

At the first light of dawn, we crept up on the still waters.

While the three serious fishermen had already cast and recast and cast again, catching naught but weeds, I finally got my line untangled, reluctantly mashed an uncooperative worm around the hook, and gracelessly slopped the baited line into the water.

POW! A strike! Reeling in, I found a very small fish. How small? "I've-never-seen-anyone-catch-a-fish-that-small" small. What do I do with it? "Take the hook out of its mouth and throw it back."

Tearing the hook out of the gasping mouth of this baby fish was not something I had been told about. What a terrible thing to do to a living creature. Once was enough. I'm thinking maybe if I just cast the line in with no bait on it, I won't catch anything and won't have to get into hook-tearing-out-abuse again. Save face. Just pretend to fish.

Second cast. *POW!* Another strike!

I reeled in. A bat. Yes, a b-a-t. A tiny b-a-t, hooked by its wing. I had somehow snagged it in midair and drowned it while dragging it through the water.

"What's the limit on these?" I asked my fellow fisherfolk, holding the bat for them to consider. The matter was passed down the lake for judgment.

"My uncle caught a bat."

"A what?"

"Ask your father what to do."

"Mr. Fulghum caught a bat and wants to know what to do with it."

"A *what*?"

They gathered around: "We've never seen anyone catch a bat."

They were awed.

And annoyed.

We had not come to fish for bats. This was fooling around.

After tearing the bat loose from the hook, I

buried it. And decided that fishing was not part of my karma. Not everyone is supposed to be a fisherman.

Sitting alone over in the campground, I ate my ration of trail gorp, throwing a walnut or two toward the ground squirrels hanging around our campsite. To have something to occupy my time, I took the hook off my line and tied a walnut on the end and cast the bait toward a squirrel. Who promptly swallowed it. *POW!* I had caught a squirrel! Reeling him around the campsite, trying to get him close enough to get the walnut and line out of him, I attracted the attention of my nephew, who passed the latest news down the lake.

"My uncle is fishing for ground squirrels—he just caught one."

"A *what?*"

And here they came in a cloud of dust and disbelief.

It was a long ride home. I, having degraded the fishing trip with unwarranted frivolity, kept my mouth shut. And they, having caught nothing— *nothing*—not a bite—were in no mood to talk. It didn't help when I said we should stop at the "U-Ketch-Em Trout Pond and RV Campground" to make up for our failure.

We should have brought some dynamite.

215

*I*N ART CLASS, WE HAD A MONTHLONG SESSION EV-
ery spring called "People Parts." Teams of three
students would rotate turns being artists and
model—one sitting still and the other two sitting
up close, concentrating on drawing one physical
feature at a time. Looking carefully—one item
per day—eye, nose, ear, thumb, lip, eyebrow,
tooth, hair, and elbow. We moved on to collar,
button, jewelry, belt buckle, shoelace, and big
toe.

This exercise was a prelude to drawing portraits.
It eased the students over a mental hill when they
found they could draw small parts with competence. Drawing a whole person all at once became
a less intimidating task.

* * *

The models were always reluctant. Adolescents are painfully self-conscious.

Close scrutiny made my students most uncomfortable.

"I don't want to be drawn."

"Why?"

"I'm ugly."

"They'll draw my pimples."

"My teeth have braces, and I look awful."

"I hate my nose—I don't want to think about it."

However, for the sake of art and the fear of not getting a good grade, the students usually went along. Faces were the big problem. After we got beyond the face, we cruised along. Hands were OK. As were elbows—most had never really considered an elbow—theirs or anyone else's. Raw knees were funny—and knees with faces painted on them, hilarious. The back sides of knees were interesting—hard to see your own.

Toes were trouble. Girls were very anxious about exposing their feet. Taking shoes and socks off in a classroom somehow seemed a little risqué. The girls thought their feet were ugly—and, frankly, many were. Already at sixteen, fashion had done its awful work: Their toes were bunioned and deformed; their heels were scarred and callused. To an artist, interesting—to a girl, embarrassing—to a boy, repulsive. On the other hand, while boys' feet were easier to look at, too often the smell was too strong to keep students concentrated on drawing for long. Suspending prejudice is the hardest part of drawing.

The "People Parts" project came to a mutinous halt one May day when I suggested we draw navels.

It was, after all, a school-picnic day, and the students were in shorts, T-shirts, halter tops, and even bathing suits, since an all-school water fight was a feature of the picnic. Many navels were already apparent.

Besides, we had never considered navels before. Neither I nor they had ever seen a detailed drawing of a navel. Now we were talking creativity, or so it seemed to me.

And we were also talking rebellion. No way! Students blushed. Hands covered exposed navels. "Nobody's looking at my navel. Not even me."

"This is a sick idea—what will my mother think if I come home with a drawing of my navel and stick it on the refrigerator?"

I thought his mother might be pleased that he remembered his connection to her, but his mind was made up. No.

And that was that. No volunteers.

I had ventured over into weirdness beyond toleration. And the students weren't the only opposition. In the faculty room, I raised the issue and asked a colleague, "Would you be upset if I asked to see your navel so I could draw it?"

The usually noisy faculty room was suddenly silent.

After some nervous laughs and a few smart remarks, the subject was clearly tabled as being irrelevant, stupid, and "just a bit personal, don't you think?"

What is it with navels? What do you think of yours?

If we were to take a picture of yours and put it up on a wall mixed in with the pictures of the belly buttons of a hundred other people, could you identify yours?

I asked my doctor.

Even she was a little perturbed. And no, she wouldn't show me hers.

She did say that once the umbilical scar had healed properly during the first months after birth, medical science was done with it. There are no known diseases of the navel, and it has no part in sex or waste disposal. Doctors never check it, even during the most complete physical exam. On rare occasions, after abdominal surgery or injury, or to tidy up a really ugly one, cosmetic plastic surgery is performed on a navel, but that's about it.

"Could it be surgically removed?" I asked.

In all her years of medical education and practice as a doctor, this question had not arisen. "Wouldn't that offend your mother?" she asked.

"That's kind of what I had in mind."

* * *

In the interest of education and the scientific method, the next time I was alone taking a bath, I got a hand mirror and contemplated my navel.

It's the mark of mortality.

Considering its implications is like considering my own death.

I'm not sure I believe what I know.

Here's this common scar. This unambiguous mark of mammalian creatureness—evidence that I am part of the great evolutionary chain of being that stretches back and back millions of years.

Here's this undistinguished archaic reminder that life comes from life—people are made inside people and are cut free to become persons.

The battle scar of the struggle for existence itself.

The people's purple heart.

There is a Yiddish blessing used by Jews to acknowledge this commonality.

"A gezund dir in pupik." An easygoing blessing.

It means "Good health to your belly button."

There is an earthy, unblinking candor here.

A wry, ridiculous, all-encompassing wish that you should be in wonderful condition from the very center of your being. So be it, Amen.

FROM THE PERSONAL FINITUDE OF NAVELS TO AN IN-
finite universal.

3.14159265358979323846264338327950288419 7 and so on,
and on, and on.

Pi or π. The number of times that a circle's di-
ameter will fit around its circumference. Or, in
other words, the distance around the outside of the
circle divided by the distance across the middle of
the circle.

So far as we know, this ratio cannot be calculated with perfect precision.

So far, no pattern emerges in the endless parade
of digits.

Pi, therefore, is a transcendental number.

* * *

I am not now, nor have I ever been, a mathematics enthusiast. But given this information in junior high school, I felt I had been handed the end of the fine thin string that was attached to infinity. This was not math, it was metaphysics.

In ninth grade, I entered a contest to see who could memorize the longest extension of pi. I got as far as thirty-nine decimal places. And took third place. Even now, somewhere in the filing cabinets of my head, thirty-nine places of pi remain—still attached to the inconceivable.

The infinitude of pi has intrigued students of mathematics for almost four thousand years. The earliest written record is on a papyrus scroll from Egypt from about 1650 B.C..

In the seventeenth century, Ludolph van Culen, a German mathematician, calculated pi to thirty-five decimal places—a remarkable feat if all you have to work with is your head and a pencil and paper. Pi absorbed his mental energy for most of his life, and was so important to him he had it carved on his tombstone.

Though it is suspected that there is no pattern in pi and never will be, the hunt continues now that we have the power of supercomputers at our command. A trillion digits is possible. Working at 100 million operations per second, the latest achievement is 2 billion 260 million 336 digits, ending in

9896531. Printed in a single line, the number would reach from Seattle to Miami. Looking very carefully, you will still see no pattern that suggests an end.

So what? Who cares?

Those who want to know what's beyond present knowledge.

Those who wanted to know what the back side of the moon looked like.

Those who are driven by the same curiosity that launched the orbiting telescope, the Mars biosphere, cell engineering, cancer research, and the project to contact intelligent life in outer space. The same spirit that investigates belief in an afterlife and the nature of God.

Those who believe there *just must be an explanation*.

We are not comfortable with untidy solutions and loose relationships. We want an existence built around a binary code. Yes or no. Black or white. True or false.

Much of the machinery of our time is binary.

The expression of most phenomena can be reduced to complex sequences of on-off, open-shut, yes-no dichotomies. The language of the computer upon which I am writing at this moment is based on a binary code. In the standard convention, each letter of the alphabet has an eight-bit code of ones and zeros.

Same as with Morse code of telegraph days—dot or dash. And now the thick/thin bar codes for product pricing. Something or nothing. Being or nonbeing. Yin or yang. Even in Biblical days, decisions were made in the temple with two stones, the Urim and Thummin, cast to determine the will of God.

Pi doesn't fit the program here. It's a tangible star trek—a bridge between the known and the infinite. It is a puzzle that exists anywhere in the universe where round things exist. From the shape of planets to waves of energy in far space to the spiral of living DNA to the circle of the lens of the human eye and the shape of each person—the perfect roundness of the single egg each of us once was—just before the moment of conception. All a matter of pi. The elegant mystery of the relationship between *around* and *across* acting in concert.

Will we ever find a repetitive pattern to pi?

Will we ever exactly know the nature of God?

With ultimate questions, the answers always seem to hang in the balance.

The answer is always the same. . . .

*I*T IS THE YEAR 2050. IN A LARGE EASTERN EURO-pean city—one that has survived the vicissitudes of more than a thousand years of human activity—in an open square in the city center—there is a rather odd civic monument. A bronze statue.

Not a soldier or politician.

Not a general on a horse or a king on a throne.

Instead, the figure of a somewhat common man, sitting in a chair.

Playing his cello.

Around the pedestal on which the statue sits, there are bouquets of flowers.

If you count, you will always find twenty-two flowers in each bunch.

The cellist is a national hero.

* * *

If you ask to hear the story of this statue, you will be told of a time of civil war in this city. Demagogues lit bonfires of hatred between citizens who belonged to different religions and ethnic groups. Everyone became an enemy of someone else. None was exempt or safe. Men, women, children, babies, grandparents—old and young—strong and weak—partisan and innocent—all, all were victims in the end. Many were maimed. Many were killed. Those who did not die lived like animals in the ruins of the city.

Except one man. A musician. A cellist. He came to a certain street corner every day. Dressed in formal black evening clothes, sitting in a fire-charred chair, he played his cello. Knowing he might be shot or beaten, still he played. Day after day he came. To play the most beautiful music he knew.

Day after day after day. For twenty-two days.

His music was stronger than hate. His courage, stronger than fear.

And in time other musicians were captured by his spirit, and they took their places in the street beside him. These acts of courage were contagious. Anyone who could play an instrument or sing found a place at a street intersection somewhere in the city and made music.

In time the fighting stopped.

The music and the city and the people lived on.

* * *

A nice fable. A lovely story. Something adults might make up to inspire children. A tale of the kind found in tourist guidebooks explaining and embellishing the myths behind civic statuary. A place to have your picture taken.

Is there any truth in such a parable other than the implied acknowledgment of the sentimentality of mythmaking? The real world does not work this way. We all know that. Cellists seldom become civic heroes—music doesn't affect wars.

Vedran Smailovic does not agree.

In *The New York Times Magazine*, July 1992, his photograph appeared.

Middle-aged, longish hair, great bushy mustache. He is dressed in formal evening clothes. Sitting in a café chair in the middle of a street. In front of a bakery where mortar fire struck a breadline in late May, killing twenty-two people. He is playing his cello. As a member of the Sarajevo Opera Orchestra, there is little he can do about hate and war—it has been going on in Sarajevo for centuries. Even so, every day for twenty-two days he has braved sniper and artillery fire to play Albinoni's profoundly moving Adagio in G Minor.

I wonder if he chose this piece of music knowing it was constructed from a manuscript fragment found in the ruins of Dresden after the Second World War? The music survived the firebombing.

Perhaps that is why he played it there in the scarred street in Sarajevo, where people died waiting in line for bread. Something must triumph over horror.

Is this man crazy? Maybe. Is his gesture futile? Yes, in a conventional sense, yes, of course. But what can a cellist do? What madness to go out alone in the streets and address the world with a wooden box and a hair-strung bow. What can a cellist do?

All he knows how to do. Speaking softly with his cello, one note at a time, like the Pied Piper of Hamelin, calling out the rats that infest the human spirit.

Vedran Smailovic is a real person.

What he did is true.

Neither the breadline nor the mortar shell nor the music is fiction.

For all the fairy tales, these acts *do* take place in the world in which we live.

Sometimes history knocks at the most ordinary door to see if anyone is at home. Sometimes someone is.

Most everyone in Sarajevo knows now what a cellist can do—for the place where Vedran played has become an informal shrine, a place of honor. Croats, Serbs, Muslims, Christians alike—they all know his name and face.

They place flowers where he played. Commemorating the hope that must never die—that someday, somehow, the best of humanity shall overcome the worst, not through unexpected miracles but through the expected acts of the many.

Sarajevo is not the only place where Vedran Smailovic is known. An artist in Seattle, Washington, saw his picture and read his story. Her name is Beliz Brother. Real person—real name. What could an artist do?

She organized twenty-two cellists to play in twenty-two public places in Seattle for twenty-two days, and on the final day, all twenty-two played together in one place in front of a store window displaying burned-out bread pans, twenty-two loaves of bread, and twenty-two roses.

People came. Newspaper reporters and television cameras were there. The story and the pictures were fed into the news networks of the world. And passed back to Vedran Smailovic that he might know his music had been heard and passed on. Others have begun to play in many cities. In Washington, D.C., twenty-two cellists played the day our new president was sworn into office. Who knows who might hear? Who knows what might happen?

Millions of people saw Vedran's story in *The New York Times*. Millions have seen and heard the continuing story picked up by the media.

Now you, too, know.

Tell it to someone. This is urgent news. Keep it alive in the world.

As for the end of the story, who among us shall insist the rest of the story cannot come true? Who shall say the monument in the park in Sarajevo will never come to pass? The cynic who lives in a dark hole in my most secret mind says one cellist cannot stop a war, and music can ultimately be only a dirge played over the unimaginable.

But somewhere in my soul I know otherwise.

Listen.

Never, ever, regret or apologize for believing that when one man or one woman decides to risk addressing the world with truth, the world may stop what it is doing and hear.

There is too much evidence to the contrary.

When we cease believing this, the music will surely stop.

The myth of the impossible dream is more powerful than all the facts of history. In my imagination, I lay flowers at the statue memorializing Vedran Smailovic—a monument that has not yet been built, but *may* be.

Meanwhile, a cellist plays in the streets of Sarajevo.